*Peter Haskell,*

*People with _____ _____ _____ work.*
*others. Keep _____ _____ _____*
*May this book _____ _____*
*child in your league a winner.*

# Life Lessons

### from

# LITTLE
# LEAGUE

*The future of*
*Little League is you*

*Vince*

# *Life Lessons*
## from
# LITTLE
# LEAGUE

## A Guide for Parents and Coaches

# Dr. Vincent Fortanasce
### *with a foreword by Orel Hershiser*

Image Books
DOUBLEDAY
*New York   London   Toronto   Sydney   Auckland*

AN IMAGE BOOK
PUBLISHED BY DOUBLEDAY
a division of Bantam Doubleday Dell Publishing Group, Inc.
1540 Broadway, New York, New York 10036

IMAGE, DOUBLEDAY, and the portrayal of a deer drinking from a
stream are trademarks of Doubleday, a division of Bantam
Doubleday Dell Publishing Group, Inc.

Book Design by Bonni Leon

Library of Congress Cataloging-in-Publication Data

Fortanasce, Vincent.
Life lessons from Little League : a guide for parents and coaches /
Vincent Fortanasce ; with a foreword by Orel Hershiser.
        p.   cm.
        "Image books."
    1. Little League baseball.   2. Baseball for children—
        Psychological aspects.   I. Title.
            GV880.5.F67   1995
796.357′62—dc20                                    94-39358
                                                   CIP

# *Contents*

## Section I: Do You Ever . . .

## Section II: The Name of the Game Is Character

## Section III: Harmony amid Discord

## Section IV: Life's Lessons

## Section V: Seize the Day

# Contents   ix

# Cleats in the Clay

Many years ago, on an enchanted evening, in a room lit by the glow of a fireplace, my wife Arlene and I reminisced with dear friends and a guest, who was clothed in the brown robes of a friar. The guest shared a dream with us of two pairs of footprints on a beach: one his own, the other God's. He lamented that God appeared to have abandoned him at the most difficult times in his life, as one set of prints vanished at those moments. Instead, he learned that God had carried him. He had not titled his dream, but that night we collectively came up with "Footprints in the Sand."

Arlene and I were stunned a few years later when this identical story was in every store from coast to coast, its author anonymous.

Did that experience influence my unconsciousness? Maybe it did. After my third Little League season, I, too, had a dream of footprints.

In this dream, I hovered like an eagle over the deep red clay of a baseball diamond. Strangely, there was no outfield—only an endless stretch of manicured soft clay.

Extending from home plate to the pitcher's mound were two pairs of footprints: one larger pair of an adult, and one small, with the cleated imprints of a Little Leaguer. At the pitcher's mound, the footprints suddenly multiplied. One set of large and small treked toward right field, one set toward left field, and the third toward center field.

The set heading toward right field went on a short way when suddenly the large pair of footprints disappeared, leaving only the little cleated pair to wander off aimlessly. This made me feel sad.

The set toward the left also went only a short distance when, again, the large pair vanished. At that moment, the small cleated pair stumbled and left deep rents in the clay. That made me upset and angry.

The third set of footprints, however, continued on indefinitely. At intervals, I saw the small cleated pair wander off and come back. Each time they returned, they appeared larger, until, at the end, both were the same size. This made me feel contented.

When I related this story to Arlene, she interpreted it as follows:

"The first set of prints, where the large footsteps disappeared and the little cleats wandered off aimlessly, represents those parents who bring their Little Leaguers to the field and leave. You've often said to me this makes you feel sad, because the child is without the support and guidance of his parents.

"The second set, where the little footprints stumble and leave deep rents in the clay, are those children who bear the load of their parents' unfulfilled expectations, as they carry their parents' heavy load. This makes you angry, because it's such a heavy burden for a small child.

"The third set, which remained together with the small pair at times wandering off and returning larger, are those parents who are steadfast and always there for their child. They know when to let go and allow their child to grow—and every time they do, that child matures. This made you feel content, because these parents nurtured their children to be all they can be."

# *Foreword*

## Orel Hershiser

It seems like yesterday that my dad took my hand and led me out to the Little League field. My dad managed my team and my mom attended all the games. I can see now that their attendance was more than just a physical presence at the ball field; it was their love and concern and good example of honesty and fair play, and it gave me determination and courage. These were instilled values that I only began to appreciate once I brought my own two sons to the Little League field.

Today my mom and dad are no longer there at the Little League field. But the legacy they left me will endure through me and be passed on to my children and then on to their children. The source and conduit of this legacy is none other than Little League baseball. No, Little League baseball doesn't inherently teach honesty, fidelity, and discipline in and of itself. What it does do is give us the opportunity to pass these values on in a social setting.

I believe Little League has more importance and relevance in our society today than twenty-five years ago when I played in Little League. Why? The reason is that most families now have both mother and father working to make ends meet. The children are left with baby-sitters and teachers. Though many of these people are devoted, none, I feel, can fulfill children's needs as do their mothers and fathers.

In coaching my own children, I noticed many of the boys and girls had their main or primary contact with their mothers and fathers at these games. Little League had taken on a vital role in the bonding between the children and their parents. Relationships that were once centered at home are now centered on the Little League diamond. The ages of six to twelve years are critical in the child's development. It is during this period that we as parents can have the greatest impact on them. During this brief time, we are their heroes and heroines. The sun rises and sets for our children depending on our words and expressions. It is for these reasons that Little League must be a positive experience. It should be an experience that enhances good feelings between our children and ourselves. It is for this reason that I have taken such a personal involvement in Little League. I've been the national spokesperson for Little League, and my parents were awarded Little League Parents of the Year for their involvement.

Unfortunately, my own experience in Little League has not always been positive. It is not necessarily my fault, yet sometimes I must admit that I, too, get caught up in the moment and forget the primary reason I am at the Little League field: my children. The purpose, in my opinion, is to give them a nurturing environment, to grow, to learn honesty, respect for their elders, discipline, and teamwork, and to have fun. All parents must realize that no one can win all the time and it is a rare child who will make it to the major leagues.

A fact that often saddens me is Little League parents whose main goal is to make their children professional ballplayers. They place incredible pressures and expectations on the children. The reality is that any child's chance of succeeding is less than one out of one hundred thousand players. Due to these odds, parents must be open to other possibilities for their children rather than concentrating on building just talent. It's not being the best, but trying one's best that is important. As Dr. Fortanasce says: "Losing is okay, as long as you don't lose the lesson."

To my dismay, I often saw coaches having tantrums, parents scolding their youngsters because of some trivial error on the field. Rather than encouraging their children, they tear them down, and rather than praising the good they did, they magnified their errors. Rather than teaching respect and honesty, they scorn the umps and abuse the rules to win. Parents berated their children's managers for the teams' not winning, and the coaches blamed the children. Little League baseball, instead of being a nurturing nest, became a thicket bush of malcontent. Who was to blame? Not the smiling little faces dressed in uniforms; rather, it was a few misguided adults. Adults who forgot the primary purpose of Little League is not only to build talent but to build character.

As I read Dr. Fortanasce's *Life Lessons from Little League*, the

words of his father, "Talent will get you to first base, but character will carry you home," stick out most in my mind. "Character,
courage, and loyalty" is the Little League motto.

*Life Lessons from Little League* was like a cool summer
breeze, a refreshing and innovative approach to making Little
League a positive and wonderful experience in a world so in need
of hope. It is unlike any other book I've read on Little League. I
am certain it will be a classic: its universal principles on parenting
span the generations and its concepts of sportsmanship span all
athletic endeavors, including soccer, football, hockey, and others.

You will learn about the inner world of your children—how
they think, how they understand, how they are influenced both
positively and negatively. Furthermore, you'll learn to understand
yourself and your reactions on the Little League field. "Children
will be children but parents must be so much more." One thing
my mother and father instilled in me is that children must believe
in themselves to achieve. If you believe in them, if you are there
for them on the Little League diamond, you will see it in the
sparkle in their eyes and the glow of their smiles.

After his or her parents read Dr. Fortanasce's *Life Lessons
from Little League*, there is no reason why any child should have
anything but a wonderful time in America's favorite pastime. The
feel of the clay, the fragrance of the grass, the cheerful chatter of
the Little Leaguers resonating with the crack of the bat to the
cheers of the parents, is America. This is the world of Little
League.

# *Little League's Diamond of Dreams*

Little League is where memories live,
Full of wonders only baseball can give.
It's a field where you learn,
And a place where you play,
It's a refreshing respite on a hot summer's day.

It is nostalgic, yet refreshingly new.
It is a diamond, clay red, grass green, sky blue.

Little League is where hope and imagination grow,
A diamond that brightens life with each throw,
Yes, a diamond with glittering dreams,
And sparkling moments to share.
It's coaches who listen and parents who care.

Little League is where a youngster's fantasies thrive,
Where coaches affirm each child with a "High five!"
Home runs, double plays, and stolen bases,
Peanuts and Cracker Jacks and shoes with untied laces.

Little League fills the fantasy of a child's dreams,
With laughter, cheers, and gleeful screams.
With diving catches and home runs just fair,
And "Go, batter, pitch 'er right in there."

Little League's a time when your child slides into home,
Your baby no longer, he's now on his own!
Yes, it's a moment when a cherub child's face sparkles
    and gleams,
Truly, Little League baseball is A DIAMOND OF DREAMS.

—Coach Vincent Fortanasce

# Section One

# DO YOU EVER . . .

. . . feel your heart drop down into your gut as you see how clumsy your child is compared with some of the other children?

. . . feel like a failure because your child sits on the bench half the game?

. . . wonder if your child will be a failure forever if he plays right field, ending up a janitor, with the pitcher as his boss?

. . . wonder if girls should be on the same ball field with boys?

. . . wonder why the other parents and children seem to have it all together, when you and your child do not?

. . . wonder if practicing with your child and attending the Little League games really make a difference later on—or is your job really more important?

. . . feel like pulling your hair out in aggravation when trying to teach your child to play?

# <u>2</u>  Life Lessons from Little League

. . . wonder if the look on your face tells your child more than what comes out of your mouth?

. . . feel the final blow to Little League has been dealt by mom managers?

. . . wonder if Little League is really a good experience?

Well, so did I.

# one

## The Mother of All Meetings

*You never get a second chance to make a first impression*

I glanced at my watch—6:00 P.M. The sun was starting to set behind the San Gabriel Mountains, filling the sky with the dreamy hue of dusk. I still had three patients left to see, a fistful of phone messages to return, and a stop to make at the hospital to check on a patient I had admitted that morning. Oh, anxiety, how I love it! I also had my first Little League parents meeting, for which I could not be late. I thought again about why, with my schedule, I ever took on this extra responsibility. I often burn the candle at both ends; was I trying to burn it in the middle, too? No! If I did not schedule time for my own children, who would?

I tried to hide my time predicament while seeing my last three patients. The meeting would start at seven-thirty sharp. If only I had an identical twin brother, I thought for the nine millionth time. I purposely did not look at my watch again until I jumped behind the wheel of my car in the doctors parking lot. I winced—it was seven-thirty. I flew out of there as if I were rushing to a cardiac-arrest code. I was certain all the parents would be at my house by now, waiting. What type of manager would they think I was? What kind of example would I set? I decided I had better drop the part in my speech about punctuality, or they might all die laughing.

As I often do, I carried on three conversations with myself at once as I tore through the streets. Where had I put the instruction sheet sent by the Little League president? Well, I remembered what it looked like—I would just ad-lib. Where was that list of parents' and children's names? Did I tell them seven o'clock or seven-thirty? Racing through a stop sign—or rather, making a courtesy slow down—I jotted down some quick notes. First, I would do a common-sense discussion on the developmental characteristics of Little Leaguers, followed by some neurophysiology and the neuropsychological gestalt of parent-and-child interaction, then finish up with some psychodrama and play therapy. Nah, that would never work. Even medical students fell asleep when I tried that.

Seven thirty-nine. I had made the fifteen-minute drive from the hospital to my house in nine minutes. As I opened the door, I switched my distraught facial expression to one that read, "Hiya, folks, I'm your kids' Little League manager." Instead of being greeted by a crowd of enthusiastic parents, though, I found only a handful of adults milling around the room while their little tots ran through the halls. We adults all sat down and had some stilted, quiet conversation, as if we were at a wake. Thirty minutes later, half the parents were still not present, so I got on the telephone. Those not there, however, had excuses: it was poker night, or a "bad time." Some honestly said, "You mean we have to go to the meeting to have our kids play Little League?" It suddenly dawned on me: hey, these parents think this is a babysitting service! And here I had risked getting three driving violations to be here on time—not to mention my life and those of my patients. As I continued phoning the missing parents, I looked down at the stack of notes shoved into my breast pocket—return calls I had yet to make to my patients. By eight-thirty I decided to start the meeting, even though a third of the parents had still not shown up.

That first year, I began with the topics I thought were supposed to be important—you know: shoes and pants, gum chewing, rubber cleats, the time and date of the opening ceremonies. Of course, by my second year, I realized how naive I had been. I had forgotten to spell things out, like "Make sure your child's shoes are tied," and "Make sure he or she's gone to the bathroom before practice," and, most important, "Make sure you come back to pick up your child." Though these things may seem obvious, I discovered during my first several years as manager that even the obvious needed to be spelled out, because the parents (myself included) were often not much more than grown-up kids. As the seasons passed, I found this meeting could be both a memorable and enlightening experience—enlightening because most parents entering Little League have little insight into the tremendous potential impact it can have on both their children and their family's interactions. (I've seen families grow and get divorced, right on the Little League diamond.) Little League is often the families' first real experience of son-and-father or daughter-and-father bonding. Of fifty parents questioned, forty-five mentioned their first meeting as being both the most memorable and influential on their outlook on Little League.

## Empty Chairs Have No Eyes

I realized after my first year that no matter how awe-inspiring the first meeting was, unless those chairs were filled with parents —and grandparents, uncles, aunts, or whomever else—it would have no impact. By my second year, I learned some sure-fire tactics for getting families there.

First, I had to personally call all the parents myself, and emphasize four things:

1. The children needed it;
2. They, the parents, needed it;
3. I needed it; and
4. We all needed it to keep our sanity.

I stressed that they, as parents, must first invest in their family, and then in their careers and jobs. All of us trying to make ends meet sometimes wonder which comes first, the chicken or the egg. There must be no doubt in families that the children come first, before the job. Children must not be sacrificed for any job, no matter how difficult the going gets. As the saying goes, "Where there's a will, there's a way."

By my third year, full and punctual participation was the rule, not the exception. After dispensing with the pleasantries of "Hi, what school did you go to?" and "Oh, I buy my groceries there, too," the meeting would begin.

## The Meeting

I once had a professor who said on the first day of class, "For centuries, teachers have asked, How can I gain the attention of my students? Jokes will keep some of you awake, informative lectures will keep some of you interested, and debates will keep some of you involved. However," he paused to put his hand in his brief case and pull out some papers, "an exam will keep you all awake, interested, and involved!" And so it did!

I decided to try it myself: "I want to welcome those of you who are in Little League for the first time to the beginning of a wonderful journey. As with any trip you undertake, though, you must be prepared. Is there air in the tires? Is the tank gassed up? Do you have proper clothing and enough food? Well, I have a test for you parents who are either new to the game or my team, to see if you (not your children) are prepared to embark on this journey through Little League."

At that moment, I could usually tell the type of parents I was dealing with. Some would laugh, thinking I was joking; others would begin to chew their nails. Still others would sink down into their chairs with their hands already up, looking for the bathroom.

To the surprise of those still smiling, I would smile back and say, "The first question is: What do you expect your Little Leaguer to learn from baseball?"

As I looked around, the parents' eyes would gaze off in every direction—as long as it was not mine. I always started with the one whose hand was up first, or, if no one volunteered, with the one trying hardest not to be called on—that way, I could put him or her out of misery soonest.

"Mr. Dogood, what do you think?"

After a couple of indecisive gulps, he would say, "To learn to win despite the odds." He would follow this announcement with furtive glances, looking for approval from one of the other parents. I then went around the room in an orderly fashion. The first answer was usually followed by variations on the same theme: to learn to be the best by winning, to learn to compete and win. Yes, invariably, to win is what parents first expect their children should do. With each collaborating answer, the parents' focus became more certain, and their answers more emphatic. By the time we had gone around the room, they were smugly nodding in unison, "Yes, to *win!*"

Do you agree?

If you do, you join 74 percent of the parents I polled at first meetings, who answered the same. Rather than contradict their answer, or give them one I felt was more appropriate, I would then rephrase their collective response to put it in a different light. "So, in other words, you expect your child and his or her team to beat another child, to beat another team?" Instantly, the facial expressions would turn to frowns, and the confident postures would begin to dissolve.

"Question two," I would go on without waiting for comments. "What do you think your children expect from baseball?" This was invariably followed by a curtain of silence. Kids are right—parents do not understand them. Nobody could come up with this answer. You would have thought I had just demanded a detailed account of Einstein's Law of Relativity.

I asked these questions at this first meeting to lay the foundation for the parents' concepts of Little League—since the children would be playing not only with me, but often would continue on in baseball. Why a test? In the academic field, professors know a person's memory for an item is only 33 percent one month after a test if he answered correctly, but is 73 percent if he answered incorrectly and was then corrected. We do learn better from our mistakes.

Taking a break from the quiz, I would then ask if anyone had questions of his own. I would quickly deal with giving out the times, dates, and length of the practices, so the parents knew when to drop off and pick up their children. I then asked my next quiz question.

"What should you expect from me?" These answers were usually right on the money: "I expect you to set a good example for my child."

"I expect you to teach him the basics of the game."

"I expect you to give him or her encouragement and be supportive." Some even said they expected me to love their child as they did. To be reliable, to help the child win was often the last request.

Finally, I would ask those parents who had been involved in Little League before what they first asked their children after a game, if they had not been able to attend. The all-time most common answer was "Did you win today?" The second most frequent question was "How did you do?"

Do you think this is what you should be asking?

What was my point? Simply that starting from this first meeting, I wanted my team parents to re-focus away from "I want my child to learn to win," or the pursuit of perfection, to the pursuit of contentment and confidence; from "I want my child to be the best player on the best team"—the pursuit of talent—to "I want my child to be a good sportsman"—the pursuit of character. In other words, I wanted them to think about how Little League could make a difference in their child's development—that trek through life that begins with childhood, goes through adolescence, the teen years and young adulthood, and into early child-raising years, on through senility.

The point of Little League (and the point of this book) is not to teach your child to learn to win, if what you mean by winning is scoring more runs and beating the opponent. Little League is about learning from the experience the game offers—experience that can teach our sons and daughters to enjoy playing; to learn self-acceptance; to build not just talent but, more important, character based on the principles of honesty, sportsmanship, effort, discipline, tolerance, responsibility, persistence, and gratitude. Yes, a child can inherit talent and wealth, but not character—that must be learned from the example you, the parents, provide.

At the same time, Little League is also about teaching us parents how to see the world once again through the eyes and mind of a child, and how to develop child-rearing skills we may not have learned elsewhere. The experience of Little League gives us the opportunity to recognize our children as they really are: bright, open little minds waiting to be accepted and enjoyed. Our interaction in Little League allows us to see the realities of life: we cannot change the children life gives us, but we can change our expectations of them, and accept and love them for the unique individuals they are. Not every child can be the best player, but every child can have a positive experience.

The parent who can do this is the one who ultimately accepts himself or herself. Contented parents rear contented children—or is it the other way around? Likewise, a contented coach—a coach with character—is an essential factor in getting this ball rolling.

By the way, if you are still wondering what to ask your child when he or she returns from a game, how about "Did you have fun?" or "What did you learn today?" Now let's take a look into the mind and imagination of a child.

# two

## Mindy's, Stevie's, & Vinny's Minds

*Children see what you mean from what you say*

### "Go Home"

Slowly and cautiously, Mindy approached the chalk-outlined batter's box for the first time. "Hit that ball, Mindy," her dad encouraged. A bright little white sphere, the baseball sat on the tee like a light bulb on top of a lamppost. Mindy reared back with the bat and swung. A sharp, resonant crack split the morning air as the ball darted and bounced toward Patrick, the second baseman. Patrick bent to scoop up the ball, but it bounced right through his legs into the outfield. Mindy's little legs carried her all the way to second as the right fielder picked up the ball and flung it over Patrick's head into left field. Parents jumped to their feet in jubilation. Mindy's coach began to shout orders, while the opposing coach barked and groaned at his fielders. Mindy's coach waved her to third base. The little gal had never aroused so much adulation and excitement from her coaches and the parents. She ran with all the power her legs could muster and all the determination and skill in her thumping heart. A giant grin of satisfaction crossed her face as she looked into the roaring crowd. Suddenly, as she reached third base, her coach crouched low, and with intensity and the excitement of the moment bellowed, "Go home, go home." Mindy suddenly stopped. Tears welled up in her eyes as she looked at the excited and ranting parents urging her to run home; with a bowed head she began her trek toward the parking lot.

"Time!" the umpire called. All the grown-ups were confused by Mindy's actions. Was she hurt? Had she pulled a muscle? Was she frightened by the crowd? Did she have to go to the bathroom? No! Just when she thought she was doing everything so right, she was told to *go home*. They did not need her anymore. Her little heart was broken.

Realizing what happened conjured up all sorts of sighs and empathy from the parents, but, being adults—the magicians of logic—they soon forgot the heartwarming episode and began arguing the rules of the game. Was she out for going out of the base pads, as the opposing coach argued, or should the rules be dispensed with since this was an unusual situation?

What do you think?

We adults take so much for granted concerning the use of language. Nothing demonstrates more the developmental gap between Little Leaguers and their parents and coaches than the understanding of language. The apparent misinterpretation of words often sails over the heads of these little people, just as it sometimes sails over our heads. The word *strike*, for example, means something very different to a union member than to a ballplayer, just as *ticker tape* may indicate a parade to a politician, yet have another definition altogether for a heart doctor.

## Like Da Wind

Stevie, a pleasant, dimple-chinned six-year-old with big brown eyes, eager to please, strode confidently up to the plate. As I delicately set the ball on the tee, I reminded him, "How are you going to run, Stevie?"

"Like da wind, Coach!"

*Wacko!* The ball bounced straight to the pitcher. Stevie took off like a shot toward first base. The ball, juggled by the pitcher, was now in his hands and ready to be tossed to first. Stevie, racing down the first-base pad, was no more than two steps from the bag. Parents and coaches screamed words of encouragement.

"Run, run, Stevie, run!" Suddenly, just when it appeared that Stevie had the ball beaten by five paces, he put on the brakes and almost came to an abrupt stop, no more than one foot from the bag. He stepped on the base, but not before the ump bellowed, "You're out!"

I took Stevie aside and again reminded him that he could run past first base, he did not have to stop on it. He took this well, as I had a big smile on my face, and I gave him a little pat on the back.

When Stevie came up again, we had a man on first and second. I asked him, "How are you going to run?"

A smile on his face, he said in his most determined voice, "Like da wind, Coach."

In a more foreboding tone, I asked, "Are you going to stop at first base?"

"No, sir, Coach!"

*Blam!* The ball clunked off the tee to the shortstop. The fans cheered as Stevie ran like there was no tomorrow, right toward the bag, never missing a step.

Three men on base. Attention quickly moved to Charlie. I patted him on the back. "The bases are loaded, Charlie. You know what to do." I looked at third base—there was Jennifer. Second base, Ryan. First base—*no one*. "Where is Stevie?" I yelled.

Everyone stood up. The first-base coach remembered him whizzing by. He was nowhere to be found. Wait! There was some little boy with a yellow Padres uniform running out to the tennis courts in a direct line from home plate. Needless to say, the game was delayed and Stevie retrieved, fully exhausted. If it were not for the fence, who knows where he would be today! Even I marveled. What Stevie lacked in skill, he made up for in effort.

Coaches and parents often forget the importance our words have on these youngsters. To us, they are just suggestions; to the child, they are commands to be dutifully followed. Stevie ran his little heart out, keeping his promise not to stop, but to go right past first base, forever.

### The Bionic Base Runner

Vinny, in his first game, was on first base. I crouched low to whisper that he must really turn it on, as the team needed this run. He must dig deep, and run his hardest.

Vinny's mind went into overdrive. "You bet, Coach," he said firmly.

Patrick hit a towering drive just over second base. Vinny took off like no tomorrow—but in slow motion. His knees pumped high, his fists thrust back and forth, but there was barely any movement. His tiny pet box turtle could have beaten him to second base.

As fortune would have it, the ball went past the charging center fielder. I screamed, I pleaded, I begged on my knees for him to run, but all this resulted in only a greater pumping and thrusting of little hands and feet. No! I thought as he began rounding second and going to third. He will be out by an hour! I covered my face in anguish as my son strutted toward third base. Miracle of miracles, the center fielder threw the ball over the second-base player's head, into the left-field bleachers. As Vinny reached third, I exploded with all the pent-up emotion of a bull being goaded by a red flag. "What are you doing?" I yelled.

"I was using my bionics, like Steve Austin." Steven Austin, played by Lee Majors, was TV's "Six-Million-Dollar Man," Vinny's hero. When the character turned on his bionics, he was shown in slow motion to emphasize the effort.

Children's minds interpret things literally and concretely, yet their reality is a collage of fact and fantasy. Like Vinny, they can easily confuse a television hero with their own performance on the field. They are miracles of imagination—dutiful and wanting to please, volatile, yet resilient.

# three

## Mean What You Say

*Communication is 10 percent words, 30 percent tone of voice, and 60 percent body language*

José was playing shortstop. The bases were loaded with two outs. He knew this was an important play. The batter hit a hard grounder right to him. Just as he got himself in front of the ball, it took a bad hop and went over his glove and through his legs. Two runs scored. His coach, seeing him disheartened, shouted, "Great try, José, that's getting in front of it."

What a supportive coach. Those few words of encouragement should have made José feel a little better about missing the ball; the coach knew he had tried his best. Reassurance is not what José heard, though—not when you add what I call *process*, or the way the words were delivered.

"Great try," the coach repeated, in a sarcastic and sharp tone of voice. He kicked the dirt as he shook his head disapprovingly, a look of disgust on his face. What José heard, of course, was that the coach was angry with him. He was bad, and had done something wrong, even though he had tried his best. Sarcasm hurts. It scares children and leaves scars.

Do you remember the very first communication between you and your infant? It was visual: you smiled, and the baby smiled. Next came tone of voice—you made a loud or angry sound, and the baby jumped or cried. You spoke softly or gently, and he or she cooed or smiled. Although verbal communication, or the actual words used, becomes increasingly important to children between ages six and nine, much of what they learn continues to come from the nonverbal communication of gestures, facial expressions, actions, and habits. When I was a boy in Little League, for example, my dad would tilt his hat back on his head when he was truly upset and say, "Jiminy Crickets." I dreaded it. It made me feel the same way I did when shocked by an unexpected clap of thunder. Obviously, my dread came from his tone of voice, not his words. So,

**Communication Lesson #1:** Always make sure your tone of voice and facial expressions are consistent with the meaning of your words; otherwise, children become confused and scared. Kids whose parents communicate inconsistently, their words differing from their expressions, are often less trusting of their parents, and even friends and teachers. Remember, little boys and girls have a hard enough time processing words without having to decipher the "real" message.

**Communication Lesson #2:** Never underestimate the imagination of a child. Eddy refused to get up to bat when I told him the bases were full. No matter how I pleaded and cajoled, I could not get him up to the tee. Finally, I had to substitute another player to bat for him. The next day, his parents explained that he had overheard me describe how I always choked when I had to get up with the bases full. Eddy did not want to die! Always spell things out verbally, not only in practice but during the game as well.

**Communication Lesson #3:** Spelling things out does not mean literally spelling each word; it means repeating and repeating and repeating and repeating and repeating . . . and never assuming that the children know the basics. My first-year players, for example, never remembered where first, second, third, and home were until their fifth or sixth game—after I had run each one of them over all the bases, first through home, at least two or three times each practice, and at least twice a game.

That brings us to

**Communication Lesson #4:** Never assume children—or their parents, for that matter—fully understand a word, especially one with several meanings. I will never forget Mrs. Miller. Her little boy was up at bat. When he missed the ball, I advised him to choke up. He kept the same grip, and missed the ball again. I had to tell him several more times, "Choke up, choke up," before he would change his grip on the bat. He finally did, but not before his mother came sailing out of the stands to yell at me that her son was scared enough, I did not have to continually remind him he was choking, or messing, up!

Always say what you mean, and mean what you say. When you teach a child how to hit, you do not throw curveballs at him; you pitch the balls straight, right down the middle. Your words also need to be straight and say exactly what you mean. While sarcasm, cynicism, and double meanings merely confuse children at first, eventually they lead to mistrust and, finally, to imitation. Many parents think their children "suddenly" turn into teenage monsters, when, in fact, the parents themselves have been priming their kids to talk back in the same language they have been listening to for years. As a psychiatrist, I see it all the time—parents criticizing their children for habits the children learned from them. Like father, like son—like mother, like daughter—rings true not only at home, but on the ball field as well. I must admit that after years of self-analysis, I never say "Jiminy Crickets!" like my father did. Instead, I say, "Shoot the ugly moose!"—and all three of my children hear the same clap of thunder. Whatever you say, if you say it in a sincere, warm tone of voice, your message will be understood, and your children will appreciate it. And you . . . if you don't, I assure you, you will reap the consequences!

# four

## "My Child Can't Catch": A Parent's Worst Nightmare

### *All children are perfect in their own way*

If necessity is the mother of invention, anxiety and competitiveness are the necessities behind this chapter—the anxiety I felt when I compared my child with other children; the competitiveness I saw generated by some of the "win at all costs" coaches and managers of Little League. Why would a person like myself, with twenty-one diplomas on his office wall, be anxious and competitive in Little League, of all places? Well, let me tell you of my first year.

I had volunteered to coach the Padres. I remember sitting in the dugout, gazing out to the ball field. My third baseman, Stefan, had his eyes riveted to the Yankees batter, who hit a slicing line drive down the third-base line. Stefan dove and speared the ball with his glove. Off balance, he slung a side-arm toss to Wayne, the first baseman, then quickly spanked off the clay from his trousers. Wayne, meanwhile, noting that the runner on second was on his way to third, fired the ball back again to Stefan, who adroitly applied the tag. A double play. Not bad for two seven-year-olds.

The Padres parents were in awe, as I was; Stefan and Wayne had stifled their opponents again. They were the "iron curtain," as some of the other teams had named them by mid-season. Bob Meister, Vinny Palermo, and Mike Agarian (three Padres parents) sat silently along with me in the dugout. We all smiled in fascination. We all then looked at our own little Padres, and our smiles evaporated into frowns of concern and fear. Staring up and to the left (a sign of contemplative thinking), I wondered, Is my child normal? Is he developmentally delayed? Is he brain damaged?

As I sat wondering, I remembered my dad throwing me a ball, at least ninety miles an hour, when I was six years old. I could catch it without any difficulty; I could hit the cover off it. I stared up to the right (a sign of imaginative thinking). Ah, well, the older we get, the better we were. With age comes wisdom—or is that amnesia?

The clank of the ball off the tee woke me from my daydream. Todd, Mr. Agarian's son, mechanically got in front of it. In and out of the glove, the ball was bobbled and picked up, then tossed over the first baseman's head, just twenty feet away. Todd's dad softly groaned.

Heather, of the Yanks, hit a soft pop-fly just beyond infield, out of reach of the Padres' shortstop. Mr. Palermo's son, Phillip, was playing left field. He staggered and stumbled and lunged for the rolling ball, which had now stopped in front of him. As he reached to grab it, Stefan swept it up and flung a perfect toss to Todd on second base. Unfortunately, Todd bobbled it again; by the time he had a handle on it, the base runner was standing on second with her arms folded smugly. Mr. Palermo and Mr. Agarian groaned in unison as their heads sagged down to their shoulders. I am sure they were feeling the same anxiety I was: how come my child's not like Stefan and Wayne? There must be something wrong with him, something terribly wrong!

## What Can They Really Do?

The high noon sun seemed dim that day, despite a clear sky. I shifted over to sit between Mike, my team coach (an emergency room doctor), and Stan, my office partner (a pediatric neurologist). "Stan, is there anything written on children and baseball-skills development?"

"Not that I know of, Vince," he responded.

He was right. After a definitive search through the available literature over the next few weeks, I found there was nothing to go by in judging what was "normal" for a six-, seven-, or eight-year-old in Little League. To assess what other parents felt was important, I asked 110 of them, "When one talks of Little League, what types of development do you want for your child?" One hundred percent of the respondents said motor development, as in learning new physical skills and building talent. (Eighty-five percent also said psychological development, or learning how to interact with other children; 50 percent said intellectual development, such as learning the strategy of the game; 10 percent said language development, and less than 5 percent said moral development, such as learning how to be a good sportsman or building character.)

How strange, I thought, that we have a sport like baseball—our national pastime since 1861, played by kids since its inception—yet no one has done anything to see if the children who start playing in T-ball can master the necessary motor skills, even though that is what most parents want and expect. More important, no one seemed to know if it was even safe for children six, seven, and eight years of age to have a ball thrown or hit at them.

This line of thought fueled more questions: are boys naturally more athletically talented—stronger, faster, more aggressive—at T-ball age than girls, as I had been taught, or was this just another myth in the Battle of the Sexes? What is the norm for such a youngster hitting off a tee, catching grounders at forty-five feet, fly balls at forty-five and sixty feet, and throwing a ball forty-five feet? How much better does a child get with one and two years of experience? Why are some children of the same age so much better than others? Does parental participation actually make a difference in performance? Does a coaching staff? Will an apparent lack of athletic talent at six or eight carry all the way through high school and college?

## Testing Motor Skills

I decided that somebody needed to find out the answers to all these questions, and that, since I had been well versed in experimental models (obtaining real, factual information for an experiment) throughout my sixteen years of training to be a physician, I was the logical one to do it. Primarily, I wanted to find out how well children between ages six and nine, with varying levels of prior experience:

- hit off a tee
- catch a ground ball at forty-five feet
- catch a fly ball at forty-five and sixty feet
- throw a T-ball forty-five feet.

For statistical purposes, I gave each child five attempts in each category.

A simple task, right? Wrong! I had no trouble with the children, of course. My problems were all with the parents.

I chose a day in March that was, like any other day in Southern California, sunny and warm. I looked at Ryan sitting contentedly on the bench with all the other T-ballers. They all sat intently, each with a little gleam in his eyes; they were all ready to have fun. Ryan and his parents were the typical easy-going, type-B-personality family—ever ready to help. Ryan himself was the type of boy who was ready to play any position I placed him in; he was never whiny, pushy, or crying to get to bat first. His father, an engineer at a nearby space lab, did not have a mean bone in his body. In his second year in T-ball, Ryan was a good, confident, seasoned player.

I had thrown a hundred balls to Ryan the year before with his parents looking on. That day, though, I announced I would be testing each child to assess his or her motor coordination. Yes, I said the word *test* to the parents—the big, four-letter *T* word that evokes such awful memories and recurring nightmares. For my group of professionals, all ambitious parents, 4.0 is a very important number. Their children always get straight *A*'s—nothing less is tolerated.

I tossed a routine grounder to Ryan; it went in and out of his glove. His dad yelled, "Get in front of it, son." I threw the second ball, counting to four seconds to make sure each toss was approximately the same speed. Due to a bad hop, it went through Ryan's legs. His mom blurted out in a high-pitched voice, "Ryan, wake up! What's the matter with you? You never miss such easily thrown balls!" As the third ball was tossed, Ryan's posture became rigid, as if he were turning to stone. The ball hit his leg and bounced off—not with enough force to hurt, just enough to make him cry.

In a matter of only a few minutes, Ryan's parents had done a good job of projecting their fears of failure and expectations of perfection onto their son. I thought, Hey, this is therapeutic—at least I am not alone. You see, I had images of my own kids in wheelchairs, crippled, selling pencils on the corner with beggars' tattered gloves. These thoughts would prance through my brain whenever I noted that my son could not catch like Stefan or Wayne. I am sure Ryan's dad must have been saying to himself, How will he ever get through first grade with catches like that, no less a Ph.D. in nuclear physics! By the time my first attempt at testing was over, I realized I had done a pretty good job myself—I had destroyed one little family group and instantaneously turned their B-type, low-keyed personalities into A-type, anxious, aggressive ones.

Meanwhile, a friendly psychologist leaned over to me and whispered, "Did you see that, Vince? Definitely from a stressed family; they could use some therapy."

Professionals, I love them. They are always so ready to classify others' normal stress reactions and tribulations as sick pathology —"seriously in need of therapy"—until it is their turn to be the patient! Mr. Psychologist became so uptight when it was his child's turn that a ton of Valium might have weighed him down, but still would not have shut him up or stopped him from criticizing his son. Ah, yes, I thought, observing his reactions—in need of therapy himself. I soon found that all these parents' reactions were normal. I decided to obtain my player information during a regular practice, thus taking the stress out of the test.

## Survey Results

Q: Is it safe for a child of six or seven who has never played baseball before to catch a fly ball at forty-five or sixty feet?

A: No. Sixty percent of the girls and 45 percent of the boys tested would clearly be hit by the ball. Many who completed the task instinctively got out of the way to avoid being hit. My conclusion: never use a regular baseball with newcomers to Little League; use a tennis ball instead. A child injured at the beginning of the season may not learn to catch at all, due to fear of the ball. In fact, the number-one fear in my evaluation of farm-team Little League players was being hit by a pitched ball.

Q: Why did 15 percent more girls get hit?

A: Because of a truth known by any parent who has had both a boy and a girl: girls pay attention better at this age and tend to be more obedient. If you tell them to catch the ball, they will stand there and try to catch it.

Q: How well can children of this age hit, catch ground balls, and throw?

A: Six- and seven-year-olds batting off a tee have a fifty-fifty chance of hitting the ball beyond the eighteen-foot perimeter used for "fair" in T-ball, and a 20 percent chance of hitting a fly out of the infield, with no statistical differences between boys and girls. Ground balls were caught 40 percent of the time, dropped 40 percent of the time, and missed completely 20 percent of the time. Catching grounders was safe for all children; catching the heavier T-ball was easier than catching the tennis ball, as it gave a truer bounce that could be anticipated, and stuck in the glove better. Boys six and seven could throw a distance of forty-five feet with ease 60 percent of the time, with 40 percent accuracy. Girls could throw a distance of forty-five feet with ease 30 percent of the time with 60 percent accuracy. Basically, boys threw farther overall, but girls were overall more accurate.

After one year of experience, 80 percent to 90 percent of the children could catch a fly ball at forty-five feet. However, only 50 percent of the fly balls were caught at sixty feet, while 80 percent of the grounders were caught consistently.

After two years' experience, close to 100 percent of the players could catch fly balls at forty-five feet, 80 percent to 90 percent could catch them at sixty feet, and 100 percent caught ground balls correctly.

Q: Why are some children so much better than others?

A: I found four clear reasons:

1) Living in a neighborhood with many other children who play baseball (most significant factor)

2) Having older siblings who play baseball

3) Having a father or mother who spends a considerable amount of time teaching them baseball

4) Natural talent. Some children physically mature faster than others; others are born with better eye-hand coordination. I differentiate between these two (maturation and natural coordination) because as a child matures, becoming larger and stronger, his abilities appear to improve. Other children will catch up to him later, when their own bone and muscle development occurs. Dr. Ysuiri, the physician who examines all the Little League World Series participants, says he can predict the winners in 90 percent of the cases just by examining them for physical maturity. He predicted the winner of the 1994 World Series in a personal conversation with me a week before the games.

Q: Does parent participation at Little League games count?

A: One season, I chose six children whose parents came to the games inconsistently. When their parents were in attendance, these children got 122 hits. When their parents were not at the game, they had only seventy-five hits. In one small study, thirteen home runs were hit with a parent there, and only two when the parents were not there. I think parent participation counts a whole lot.

Q: Does a coach's attitude make a difference in a child's development?

A: According to the statistics of returning players, yes.

What I learned at the end of eight years of statistical observation is that motor development in Little League is only a small part of becoming a talented player. The major ingredients children need to enjoy Little League and have a "winning" experience are discipline, consistency, enthusiasm, and parental support, all of which build something else as well: character. A child, or adult, will only go so far on talent. If he does not develop character with that talent, he will eventually fail and become a has-been, or worse, an also-ran. If he develops character, talented or not he will become contented, independent, and, eventually, successful. Character, not talent, is the foundation—the essential building block of the right stuff.

## Battle of the Sexes

In my first year (1982) as a manager, I was assisted by none other than my dad, who had coached me in Little League thirty years earlier in New York. He was right out there on the field with me that first day of practice. When I showed him the lineup of players, he groaned. "Girls playing Little League? Since when? Are they trying to get these little girls hurt?"

I, too, brought up in the age of dinosaurs, was sorely disappointed. I had not one but three girls on my team. My dad said, "At least the dugout will be kept clean." No, he was not a chauvinist; he was just seventy years old and having a difficult time with a changing world.

His remarks, though, led to yet more questions for my statistical analysis. Should the girls keep the dugout clean while the boys keep the bases full? Are boys naturally faster? Do they catch and throw better? Are they more aggressive? Do they learn athletic skills easier because of male hormones? Does natural selection make them bigger and stronger at T-ball age? Should little girls even venture out on the same field, or are we putting the "delicate little creatures" in the lion's den, the den of the men?

My results, to the chagrin of any male chauvinist, handily showed that six- and seven-year-old girls tended to be a tad faster in the forty-five-foot trek from home to first base, while boys threw farther, although less accurately. By age eight, there were no statistical differences between their hitting and catching scores when prior practice or experience was eliminated, but the differences in throwing increased in the boys' favor. Boys also had an experience edge, as they tended to play ball with friends or their dads more often than girls did. Those girls who had fathers or brothers to practice or play with, however, did equally as well as the boys in catching and hitting, and tended to be much easier to teach. The last male/female myth finally bit the dust when I realized that the girls were, at least initially, every bit as aggressive as the boys.

After seeing everyone play the first game of the season, my dad made up the batting order. Yup! Rachael was third and Mary was cleanup. Dad may be in his seventies and a bit old-fashioned, but he was not dumb. Those two girls were the best I coached in my twelve years of Little League, and the heart and fire of my first team's lineup. My second year I was gravely disappointed to see I had only one girl on the team.

## Section Two

# THE NAME OF THE GAME IS CHARACTER

*"What lies behind us and what lies before us are tiny matters compared to what lies within us."*
**—Morrow**

Not every child can have "great talent," but every child can have great heart, hope, and character. Parents have the strongest effect on their children from infancy to twelve years of age. During this time, children's minds are like newly fallen snow. Be careful what you teach them, for every mark will show.

# five

## The Right Stuff

*Your character—not your talent—*
*is your destiny*

When I first started in Little League (though I would never admit it at the time), I envied those fathers with talented sons. You know, the kids who were born with gloves on their hands and the eyes of an eagle, who had the speed and grace of a panther. They were destined for success. Their dads only had to sit back and watch their kids perform and succeed. Right? No, wrong, I learned. Why were not—are not—talent and good looks enough? The answer lies in normal human psychological development.

### A Brief Lesson

Our self-perception is what makes us what we are, and often determines our ultimate fate. At times, we all attempt to fool the world by reflecting just the cover of our book, but what always shows through are the pages themselves. We all know of movie stars and mentally gifted individuals who feel inferior despite their beauty and intelligence. On the other hand, we also know people who appear ordinary both in appearance and intellect, yet exude an air of self-satisfaction and confidence. They seem to be made of the "right stuff."

This right stuff is what separates those individuals who do not quit when the going gets tough from those who do. The person who imagines himself a failure often lives down to that expectation; the one who believes in himself often eventually succeeds.

Can we, as parents, influence our children to cultivate the right stuff? Can we inspire them to have confidence in themselves and succeed? Yes—but only if we understand how this right stuff gets instilled and nurtured in a child. We must also understand, though, how the "wrong stuff"—insecurity and fear—gets stamped into our child's development as well. *Not only must we know what to do, but—just as important—we must know what not to do.*

## Parents: You Have One Chance

Parents and other significant adults are the most influential forces in a child's life from infancy to age twelve. After that, peers —siblings, close friends, acquaintances, etc.—take over as being the most important sources of positive or negative feedback. Actual abilities or talents are important throughout development but are often not appreciated until the teen years, or later. Sometimes they are not fully appreciated until the child has left the influence of his or her family.

You only have to listen to one teenager's opinion of another, or one sibling's appraisal by his brother or sister, to recognize how rare a child would have to be to evolve a good self-image on the basis of praise from peers. If positive self-appraisal is not formed by the early teens, the child will have a serious problem. This makes the formative years of T-ball and farm, minor, and major Little League so precious, and is the reason why parents and guardians (such as coaches) are so important.

Prior to age six, children are often very protected. They live in their own world with their parents, isolated from the harsh realities of competition and expectations. At six, their minds are filled with pleasantries, like wanting to wear a bright yellow uniform. Then they enter first grade, Little League, and soccer, and somehow their doting, docile parents suddenly undergo a scary change or metamorphosis, like a butterfly changing into an ugly caterpillar. One moment the parents are themselves, cheerful and loving, and the next they are filled with emotions their children cannot understand. Based on their short life experience, kids often categorize these parental reactions in the only two classifications they are familiar with: approval ("My mommy or daddy likes me, I am good") and disapproval ("My mommy or daddy does not like me, I am bad"). Approval, of course, brings repetition of the behavior. "What a poop!" said with a cheery voice brings (hopefully) a repeated performance on the potty. On the other hand, a deep, angry voice—"What did you do to my vase?"—brings trepidation, tears, a quivering chin, and (hopefully) avoidance of that behavior.

Well, here comes T-ball, and we, as adults, know the only way to become more proficient at the game is to practice. Practice, of course, takes repetition. Repetition is fostered by parental approval, which promotes continued effort. How can we exude continuous approval, though, when most six-year-old children are lucky to catch a ball dropped in their glove, or throw a ball within ten feet of their forty-five-feet-away target? They are going to make a lot of mistakes; if every time they make one they get a negative response, we can hardly call this a positive experience. We have to find a way, therefore, to make these "errors" (which is what they are called in baseball) into something positive.

## Positive Parenting Beyond Kindergarten

When your child attempted to take his first step but failed, did you scold, "Naughty child, you fell," or did you smile and say, "That's great, your first step"? Nobody chides a toddler for his uncertain first steps, just as nobody corrects the diction, articulation, or tone of voice of a baby's first words. Even if the sounds come only close to being a word, the house sings with ecstasy. I remember my son saying his first word, *Daddy*, as he looked at a picture of a dog. I had repeated the word hundreds of times, hoping he would say it correctly. Was I angry that he called the dog his dad? Of course not! I ran around the house as if he had won the Pulitzer prize for journalism.

Finding the good in a person, despite his errors, is called unconditional positive regard, or positive reinforcement. We all did this for our children during their formative years. What stops us, then, from using the same unconditional positive regard when they get to Little League?

Us—we stop ourselves, with our own adult conflicts, our own adult expectations, and our adult fears. Burdened by the past, preoccupied with the future, we forget the present and stop being positive, finding only the negative, the "have to change or fix" in everything our children do. Remember, your children will always be looking at you as an example of how to behave. Don't let them down!

## Parental Expectations

"One comes in contact with one's true self through one's children," claims the old adage, and sometimes, this can be really scary. We teach our children to be who they are by being who we are—and then, we often deny our own part in the process: "Where the hell did he learn to say that crap? It must have been from one of those dirty children at school."

We all have adult expectations of our children. Those expectations come from a combination of whom we think they should be, and whom we think we are or should be. Most parents fall into one of four categories, divided by expectation. I call the first the unfulfilled, or "I Coulda," parent: "My child represents what I always wanted, but did not have the opportunity to be. He will not be a laborer like Dad; I will make him a million-dollar bonus baby." This is typical of most of us.

The second is the "Overachiever" parent: "My child is representative of what I am. How dare he let his genetic lineage of excellence down! He can do better than that, and I will prove it!" This is often typical of the "guys in charge," such as professional individuals who own businesses or companies, or lawyers, executives, and foremen. Also in this category are the "Fantasy Life" parents, who imagine themselves the mothers or fathers of a famous and exceptional child.

The third type of parent I call the "Know-It-All-Blame-It-All": "My child must be what I imagine I am, but am not." This last category could be any of us. Unfortunately, parents in this category most often do not recognize their own attitudes. These moms, dads, and coaches are the saddest of all. Since they cannot accept themselves, they cannot accept their child. Even more unfortunately, these "Blame-It-All" parents find a million excuses and rationalizations for why their child did not shine today—and blame it on whoever is closest. Unfortunately, that is usually their own child.

Oh—a fourth category exists for the perfect parent. If you are one of these, move yourself to the third category.

## A Little Bit of Them All

In my experience, the parents in categories one and two are generally easy to work with. God help the child of a type three parent, though, and the coaches who have to deal with them! Many of us are a combination of all three types—in fact, I believe we all have a little of each type within us. The trick is to figure out our strongest type, then try not to let it get in our children's way.

# SIX

# The "Blame-It-All-Know-It-All" Parent

*Some people are alone because they build walls instead of bridges*

I took a long, deep breath and let the warm spring air cleanse my lungs. It was the first practice of the Little League season, my seventh and probably last year managing T-ball. I closed my eyes to listen to the innocent chatter of the players. The chirping of the sparrows seemed to complement their gleeful squeals, interspersed with the deeper warm tones of the moms and dads. Suddenly, my oneness with nature was interrupted.

"Dr. Fortanasce, I presume?" I opened my eyes and blinked against the sun.

"I am Bradley Burnham, father of Brandon." Before me stood a fortyish, mildly plump gentleman with a starched white shirt, bow tie, and, yes, black-and-white high-top sneakers.

"I have heard you have an excellent reputation. That is why I elected to have my son Brandon on your team." Well, I thought, he has good taste in coaches, if not in clothes.

"I understand from my wife, Marian, that you expect parental participation," Mr. Burnham enunciated in a British accent, "so I am here to reassure you of our thorough, unequivocal support. I have been practicing with Brandon, and I assure you, he will be more than a credit to your organization. In fact, Brandon said to me just now on the way to the field, 'Dad, I will be the best.' "

"Thank you, Mr. Burnham." As I extended my hand in friendship, I felt a slight tug in my gut.

"Okay, lads," I called to my team. (I had spoken to Mr. Burnham for only one minute, and he had already rubbed off on me.) "All the first-time players out to the field."

Mr. Burnham took this command literally and went out to the field with his son. As I began my introductory directions, I noticed him order several of the children off the shortstop position he had deemed his son's terrain.

I started by throwing soft ground balls to each child to assess his abilities. Brandon very mechanically got in front of his ball and bobbled it. When he finally caught it, he threw it awkwardly in the direction of first base. He immediately cringed, his shoulders sagging. His father then openly criticized his catch-and-throw as ". . . inadequate and, quite frankly, inferior to your potential." My stomach churned once again. The child had cringed before his father ever spoke! My own rating, according to my motor-skill experience, was that Brandon had average capability and possibly good potential.

I next ordered the children in for batting practice. Mr. Burnham was again right on me, explaining how he had played professional soccer, and how his son would, with proper coaching, follow in his footsteps. He quickly appraised me of the foul experience he had previously had with an inadequate manager who neither took advantage of, nor developed, his Brandon's exceptional potential. The volume of friendly background chatter seemed to mute and the sun to dim as I realized my season with Mr. Burnham had just begun. My mentor in psychiatric training had once said, "Pay attention to your gut feelings, Vince." All of ten minutes had gone by with Mr. Burnham, and my gut was screaming out loud and clear—trouble! I popped two Rolaids.

By the third practice, Mr. Burnham had berated the condition of the field when his son missed a ground ball, blamed the other children for disturbing his son's concentration, and made a num-

ber of remarks about the "bloody manners" of his son's teammates. By game time, Mr. Burnham had already decided that the
coaching staff favored other children and was not recognizing his
son's talent. Unfortunately, Brandon was the one who took the
brunt of his father's unfulfilled expectations; Mr. Burnham openly
railed at the little tyke, yelling and chastising him. He added a
new meaning to the phrase "child abuse." He may not have been
hitting and scarring the boy's skin, but he was making deep rents
in his psyche. Although there were many incidents with Mr. Burnham over the course of the season, one I will always remember
occurred in the second game.

We were short an umpire, so Mr. Burnham had volunteered to
take second base. By coincidence, his son just happened to be
playing second base as well. The batter hit a soft pop fly to second. Trembling, Brandon positioned himself to catch it. I remember praying he would, because I so feared his father's reaction.
The ball seemed to take forever to come down. When it did, it
careened off the tip of Brandon's glove and glanced off his chin.
Stunned, Brandon turned and cried, holding his hands over his
face. Time was quickly called. With tears streaming down his pink
cheeks, Brandon reached out toward his dad to be comforted.
Horrified, Mr. Burnham literally pushed him away and loudly reprimanded him for crying in front of everyone. I heard a collective
gasp from the watching adults, who were obviously as startled as
I at Mr. Burnham's reaction. I had to intervene and take Brandon
off the field. As he sobbed deeply on the bench, I sat down next to
him and placed a fatherly arm over his tiny heaving shoulders. He
immediately threw my arm off, then yelled at me for placing him
in a position where the sun made it impossible for him to catch
the ball.

Meanwhile, a fight had ensued on the field. Mr. Burnham had
called the batter out due to the infield-fly rule. No one could
convince him there must be someone on base to call the infield-
fly rule.

## Hallmarks of the "B-I-A-K-I-A" Parent

Mr. Burnham and his son demonstrate three essentials of the Blame-It-All parent: blame-blame-blame, or "That is not me; I did not do it; You did it!" In psychological terms, this is called 1) denial, 2) suppression, and 3) projection.

Denial is typified by the words "That is not me." Mr. Burnham refused to recognize, and in fact actively denied, the truth: his son was an average player, and he, the father, was an average-talent (to be generous) adult.

Suppression is typified by the "I did not do it" claim. Mr. Burnham suppressed his own desires by refusing to distinguish between his needs and those of his son. He had to have his son succeed at all costs due to his own perceived shortcomings. His continual criticisms were meant to tell everyone that it was his son (not him) who wanted to be "the best"; it was his son (not him), therefore, who was letting everyone down.

"You did it" indicates projection. Mr. Burnham projected—that is, blamed—any shortcoming or mistake on everything and everyone else: the condition of the field, the sun, the coaches, the other players.

Mr. Burnham had never accepted himself, and therefore could never accept his child. This is so typical of a Blame-It-All parent. It was obvious to me and anyone else who saw him run, for example, that he would have had a hard time bowling, much less being a soccer star. The Blame-It-All's characteristics of denial and projection often lead to frequent confrontations with coaches, umpires, and other parents. Blame-It-All parents use manipulation and dissension to force their distortion of truth or reality onto others, who will not simply accept it, as their child must. Unfortunately, their ultimate opportunity for manipulation comes when they turn manager, which, just as unfortunately, they often do—as did Mr. Burnham. The hallmarks of their teams are winning at all costs; favoritism; berating officials, opposing teams, and coaches; projecting any shortcomings onto others; and using the rules against others while, at the same time, constantly breaking them to their own advantage. Eventually, the vice president and president of the league get badgered by a majority of the team's parents, who complain that the coach is not playing some of the children.

The characteristic words used by Blame-It-All parents are similar to the ones used by Overachiever parents, whose children are "the best," "excellent," "exceptional"; the Blame-It-All's child is all those, but with a qualified blame.

"My son is the best, but his manager stinks."

"My son is a great hitter, but did not get on base all year because of the coach."

## Dealing with the Mr. Burnhams

These parents are true pains in the butts, believe me! Unfortunately, since we all have a little of each type of parent in us, not every primarily Blame-It-All parent sticks out like the semifictitious Mr. Burnham.

How does one deal with this type of dad or mom? With great difficulty, I am afraid. I have, however, developed a three-step approach. First, I acknowledge the parent's good intentions: "Mr. Burnham, it is so clear that you love your child. Your interest in his ballplaying tells me that."

Second, I confront his behavior. "Criticizing your son, or blaming others, though, does not solve the problem of his missing the ball."

Third, I offer a positive alternative. "Since you are so concerned, try to always see the bright side of what he does, like getting in front of the ball. If you cannot think of anything positive to say, let someone else comment on his game."

When all coaxing fails, though (and it often does), I find it best to end the relationship. I have three ways of doing that, too.

In the first method, I just let him have it. "Mr. Burnham, you are an overstuffed ——head who knows —— about baseball. If you do not like how I coach, I will arrange another coach to take your ——."

My second technique is to kill him with cynicism. "Mr. Burnham, I am only a board-certified neurologist, not a professional T-ball coach. What you need is a psychiatrist."

The third way is to try diplomacy. "Mr. Burnham, I realize you are dissatisfied with your son's progress. I try my best, but I feel you need more than I can give you and your son. Therefore, I will recommend to the league president that he be placed on another team."

The first and second ways, of course, will make you feel a lot better—but the third will solve the problem for you just as well, without worsening the situation for all. Some people are alone because they build walls instead of bridges. Be a bridge builder. Do not accept the unacceptable.

# seven

## "Overachiever" Parents

*You cannot change the child that life gives you —you can change only what you expect from that child*

The other day, I was listening to one of my friends talk of his "4.0 child"—a child with a perfect *A* grade average. At any gathering of my friends, who are mostly physicians and other professionals, the only allowable number is 4.0, the only allowable letter *A*. The bragging has gone so far lately that last night I was informed that one of my friend's children had "better than a 4.0 average"—better than perfect. "I have always been shooting for that myself," I said. "If I could not make it, maybe my child will."

As you can see, I entered this social game of "Let's play how-great-our-genetic-heritage-is" very carefully. The rules are: I let you have your fantasies, you let me have mine. "Huh! Your child has better than a 4.0 average," I tried to say with admiration.

Openly challenging an outrageous exaggeration, you see, is against the social rules in my peer group. In fact, it would be considered offensive, and would probably result in my being ostracized by my peers. Of course, I could have brought the conversation to an even more ludicrous level by pushing the question, but being my own self-confident person, I decided to change the playing field instead—especially since I could not play in their ball park when it came to my kids' grades. I therefore turned the conversation toward something even better and more important than grades—baseball.

"Well," I said, "my daughter has just returned from the All-Star Games. You know, she plays shortstop and pitcher—and sometimes both positions at once." I wanted to say, "And went four-for-three with one intentional walk," because that, too, is better than perfect.

"Why, that's wonderful," exclaimed the mother of the 4.0-plus daughter in a condescending tone. "Each child does have their own place, don't they?"

Now what did she mean by that remark? I thought. Rather than challenge it and find out, I decided just to call it a draw and move on. Besides, she knew, as I did, that what we were touting was nothing but wind.

However harmless this type of social interaction is, it becomes dangerous when we forget that friendly one-upmanship is just a social game and nothing more. The reality of our children—who they really are, and what stage of development they are at—may be (and probably is) very different from our bragging. We must accept our children as they are. When we actually expect our children to live up to these glorified images that we have created in our minds and social intercourse, we take on the traits of the Overachiever parent, whose hallmark words are always superlatives: always *wonderful, gorgeous, marvelous, the best.* Fortunately, Overachiever parents are easy to recognize by the uneasy, competitive, or nauseated feeling you get from not being able to tolerate their bull. They are the ones who tend to name-drop the fine schools they went to—Harvard, Yale, Vassar, or Brown. Overachievers often have trouble relating to the concept of what they are, because, after all, they cannot help it if their child is so intelligent or talented. The truth is, children of elementary-school age seldom really care about grades, or talent, or intelligence. They are more interested in learning new skills, making friends, learning language, and a host of other wonders the world has to offer. To put it in simple terms, only an Overachiever parent would think an *A* in second-grade spelling is important.

I will never forget a conversation I had at the La Jolla Beach and Tennis Club one summer. I listened intently as one of the parents described his young son. "He's incredible. You have to see him perform, you won't believe his talent. He is so advanced for his age, really. He's unbelievable."

To find out what this Overachiever parent was really saying, use the old psychiatrist trick of substituting *I* for *he*, *me* for *him*, and *my* for *his:* "I'm incredible. You have to see me perform, you won't believe my talent. I am so advanced for my age, really. I'm unbelievable."

## Reality Grounding for Overachiever Parents

Let's face it: 99.9 percent of our children will never live up to our imagined perfection. If they were to try, 99.9 percent would most likely fail. Those that come close, or continue to try against all odds, often pay an expensive price for questing after what they eventually realize was never their goal in the first place, but their mother's or father's. In striving for the success their parents demand, these individuals gradually accumulate the symptoms and signs of stress. In their twenties and thirties, for example, they develop chronic headaches or stomach problems—diarrhea, constipation, sour stomach. In their forties and fifties, they graduate to stomach ulcers, hypertension, panic attacks, and depression. No matter what they attain, they have learned, it will not be enough; they will have to strive for more.

Clark was just such a child. His mother and father drove him to the ball game in their new Cadillac, quite a sight in the 1950s. They always parked it where everyone could see it. Their praise for their son was nauseating to most of us, and, I knew, embarrassing for Clark, too. A good-natured, quiet boy, Clark always tried to please his parents. As I look back, he was very talented, but not to the extent of his parents' accolades—especially his mother's. "Tremendous, superstar, best of the best!" Clark was fortunate to be as talented as he was, because his Overachiever parents would have accepted no less. I remember one all-star game he played as if it were yesterday. The bases were full, Clark was up to bat. At the tensest moment possible, when all was hushed in suspense, his mother stood up and yelled, "Clark, you're the best! Hit a home run, and I'll buy you a new bike!"

Clark hit the home run, as expected. He later went on to excel at the "best" high school, the "best" college, the "best" law school, and, finally, the "best" legal firm in New York. Somehow, though, no matter what Clark achieved, he never felt it was enough; he never seemed satisfied with meeting his parents' ever-expanding expectations. He led a very sad life that ended tragically.

All this starts with us, the dads and moms, when we begin to seriously expect our children to be "better than perfect"—with a higher than 4.0 grade point average, or a 4 for 3 batting average. All this can stop with us, too, just by realizing that we do not have to be perfect, and neither do our children. We need to encourage them to be all they can be, by accepting them and rewarding their efforts. Even if they fail, or bring home a *C*-average report card, they deserve a reward for their effort. Yes, it is that simple. Remember, the sure road to failure begins when you try to please everyone.

# eight

## Lost Opportunities: The Unfulfilled Parent

*We cannot live our children's lives, and they cannot heal our childhood wounds*

Harris rarely smiled. I had never seen such determination in a ten-year-old. His dad, the struggling owner of a small gas station, was always there in his uniform with grease under his fingernails and sweat on his brow—a hardworking, good man. This dad was always practicing with his son, always demanding that he try harder, be better. Harris was definitely talented. The consistency in his pitching and hitting showed hours and hours of practice. His dad, well, he was a good parent—maybe too good. Everything seemed to be life or death to him, as if every pitch his son threw, or every swing he took, determined the outcome of not only his life, but of the world.

We were playing the Dodgers one day, and Harris was pitching. As he skipped out toward the mound, he was full of enthusiasm, pounding his glove and grinning at the second baseman. I heard his dad yell out, "Remember, Harris, we have to beat the Dodgers today." His dad then proceeded to comment on every pitch Harris made. Despite this, Harris did fine for three innings; in the fourth, though, they started hitting him. His dad's strained demeanor began to crack, and he became openly critical.

"Throw harder."

"Kick that leg up."

"Spring off the mound."

"What's wrong with you?"

He was barking orders at his own son the way a drill sergeant would bark at his troops. A Russian general in frozen Siberia would have had more mercy in his voice.

The bases were loaded. Harris wound up and threw a fast ball down the center of the plate. The determined Dodger slugged it right up the middle to center field. As two runs were scored, I looked at the mound. Harris lay there cringing in pain, crying and holding his arm. His dad did not notice, because he had buried his head in his hands, as if he were watching his gas station and all his possessions go up in smoke. I ran out to help Harris. His elbow was mildly tender, but I could find no other problem. I picked him up gently and walked off the field. He whimpered, "No, I have to pitch or my dad will be hurt."

Harris's arm was not truly injured, and we both knew it. What he really feared was letting his dad down. Harris recognized how much his pitching—and pitching well—meant to his father.

## "I Coulda Been a Contender"

Some parents, after thirty to forty years of their lives, come to the sudden realization that their fantasies and self-expectations have not been met: "If I had only bought that home ten years ago . . . it's worth a fortune now"; "My brother, he was the quiet one, but smart. He got a good education. He is knocking down the big bucks now, and I don't mean the type with antlers."

I am sure you have heard these laments, if not said them yourself. Each one of us has been struck sometime in our lives by our own self-reflection. When we look at ourselves as we really are, the true meaning of life becomes apparent, seemingly at that moment. Some call it the "time of wisdom." You have probably read or heard this prayer many times before: "God grant me the serenity to accept the things I cannot change, the courage to change the things I can, and the wisdom to know the difference." Read it over again.

This sudden parental insight (or hindsight) into all those lost opportunities is probably the most frequent single cause of conflict between good-intentioned parents and their children. The children are unaware of their parents' trials and tribulations; they are untouched by such cruel realities of life as money, prestige, and power. They enter the Little League field as Harris did, with bright, wondrous, smiling faces, ready to have a good time. They come to be part of the great American pastime of baseball. Their gloves reach from their belt buckles to their socks, their uniforms seem somehow built around them like a sack on a stick, and their glistening grins are innocent. They seem so perfectly in contact with nature. Are they aware of what their first stride to home plate means to their parents? More important, do their parents even realize what it means to them? Probably not. I am certain Harris's dad did not recognize what he was doing to his son, nor how he had erased the smile from his little boy's face.

## Listen to What They Do

Tucker's dad was an old army sergeant. If he was not, he sure could have fooled me. Tucker played shortstop. He was good, possibly the best shortstop in the league. His dad had an awful lot invested in his son. Talented as he was, though, Tucker did not walk with his head erect and his chest puffed out like the king of the roost. He stood round-shouldered, as if defeated. There was a stumble to his step, a slip to his skip, and a hitch to his hop. He acted as if he carried the world on his little shoulders. Tucker, you see, had a problem: as coordinated as he was, he always seemed to twist his ankle, only to enjoy a miraculous cure several plays later. The twisted ankles occurred whenever he missed a ball—especially if it was on a play his dad considered important. After many such instances, his mother confirmed my suspicions. Why was he so accident prone? By now, it was obvious to us all: Tucker had learned his dad would not yell at him when he was hurt. He had learned he could avoid reprimand through injury.

Did Tucker's father realize what he was teaching his son? Again, as with Harris's dad, probably not. Yet both boys were giving their fathers strong warnings. Children at this age, though truthful, continue to communicate some of their most important messages in nonverbal form. We must learn to "hear" what they are saying with their bodies and faces. We must also learn to step back and distinguish our own needs from theirs. Children do not need to be perfect; they need to be content. They do not need to produce under pressure; they need to be encouraged in a positive direction. They do not need angry, biting sarcasm; they need discipline combined with positive reinforcement and praise for appropriate behavior. If we do what causes contentment, we will always see the results in our children, especially through nonverbal signs. They will have a glide to their stride, and a small skip to their step.

## Sammy and the Tigers' Coach

The Tigers' coach had some angry words with his team. If I had not known who he was talking to, I would have expected Steinbrenner's Yankees to come running out of the dugout. Instead, a small group of six-, seven- and eight-year-olds walked out with stunted steps, slumped heads, and drooping shoulders; several had tears in their eyes. The Tigers' first baseman threw a practice grounder to the second baseman; it went through the little guy's legs. The coach bellowed, "Get your head in the game, Sammy. Get in front of it. What are you afraid of, the ball hitting you?"

Sammy looked into the dirt. The first man up plunked a grounder right to—who else—Sammy. The ball, not hit very hard, took a bad bounce and hit Sammy in the stomach. Sammy picked the ball up and threw out the runner. His coach barked out, "About time you stopped something." Sammy's face reddened. He sat down on second base and began to cry, holding his stomach.

Being the only doctor on the field, I ran out and asked where it hurt. Sammy pointed to his heart. There was no mark. The ball used for T-ball is very light and generally will not cause injury, even if it hits a child in the head.

Sammy cried out, "I can't play anymore, Coach. Can I go home now?"

As I walked the child off, the coach scoffed, "This kid is a crybaby. He has to learn to take some punishment. Do you think you give up just because you're hit? I can't understand these kids."

Sammy was the coach's son.

A coach who does not understand children is like a schoolteacher who does not know the subject he is expected to teach. Understanding baseball at the T-ball, farm, minor, or major levels is not enough. The coach must also understand the physical, mental, psychological, and moral development of children. These are not seasoned veterans or professionals; they are small children with wholesome hearts and impressionable minds, who respond well to the affirmative and are easily crushed by the negative. If I had taped what some of my fellow coaches and team parents said during the course of the season and played it back to them a year later, most would be horrified. Parents need to nurture their children with warm, positive regard and acceptance, for these are the tools that will make them have the right stuff, and be contented, self-reliant, and successful later in life.

# nine

## Coaches' Expectations

*Many go through life running from something that is not after them*

### The Headlines

I strode from the dugout to the mound, tipped my cap back, and motioned to the infielders. They quickly gathered around me. It was the bottom of the ninth inning, one out, man on first and third. We were up by one run—the National Championship hung on this next play. A fly ball, and the game would be tied. Our hometown fans mumbled anxiously, causing the stadium to hum like a beehive. The tension was so thick it was smothering. In the stands, the media people hammered out their news reports, awaiting only the title. Would it be FORTANASCE, MVP MANAGER DOES IT AGAIN or FORTANASCE FAILS ONCE AGAIN? I delivered my orders. With hands on my hips, I confidently strode back to the dugout to the roar of the crowd. The pitcher, Orel, blazed a fast ball, high and outside, as I had instructed. The runner on first, as I had anticipated, was darting toward second. The catcher fired toward second base as the man on third was signaled to go home.

Orel cut the throw off from the catcher and caught the stunned third-base runner dead in his tracks. Another managerial triumph. The cleanup batter then hammered a drive to the warning track, which was caught easily by our center fielder. The game was over. The stands burst into a chant, "Fortanasce, Fortanasce," as the players carried me in triumph to the center of the field. Suddenly a gruff voice said, "Hey, Coach, wake up. You have two little kids arguing about who gets to play first base." At first startled, I suddenly realized where I was. My visions of notoriety and an adoring public vanished.

Expectations, expectations. Was this why I had said yes to coaching the Padres team?

As a coach or manager, you must sometimes wonder, as we all do, whatever possessed you to accept the great responsibility of guiding and directing a Little League team. Many claim, "I did it only because no one else wanted the position. It was either do it, or the children don't play." Some do it for "my kid"; still others find it a challenge, something they have always wanted to do. For me it was tradition. My dad coached me when I was a child. I just naturally expected to do the same for my children.

No matter how you come about the position—voluntarily, by default, or through guilt—once you are there you have your own expectations. Like mine, these expectations are both conscious and unconscious. My conscious expectation was to coach a championship team. My unconscious expectation involved the fear of failure—FORTANASCE FAILS AGAIN in the headlines.

When you are a manager, you have more than just your own expectations to worry about. Every coach must contend with parental and team expectations and feelings of success or failure—and all of these are ultimately directed at you. "My child did not have a good experience because the coach stunk"—I have heard that remark at least a million times. Of course, they were referring to some other coach than me!

Just imagine: you have at least thirty individual parents with conscious and unconscious expectations of their son or daughter—and you. You also have to contend with all the expectations of the opposing manager, coaches, and teams; often, these set up severe conflicts. Put them all together, and you have expectations running rampant even before the season begins! Any veteran manager or coach will tell you that a competitive opposing manager is enough to kindle latent pride and hostilities in even the most gentle and docile coach. If you are already a fierce competitor in life, Little League can bring you to the brink of insanity and make you say and do things you thought only crazy people did. You could easily end up as so many of us have in the past—mature and educated adults in real life, but jumping up and down in a tantrum on the baseball field, with as many as one hundred other parents and thirty children looking on, wondering who is the adult and who is the kid.

## Bloopers I Have Known

"What are you afraid of?" gruffed Mr. Gardner, a slightly beer-bellied, five-nine, balding, hard-driving coach. Sweat dripped off his red neck in the hot noon sun. With a small bat riveted to his right hand, he threw another ball with his left and chopped down on it fiercely, causing it to bite into the dry clay and shoot toward the second baseman. He bellowed, "Get in front of it. We don't need no chickens on this team."

*Pow!* A shot to the left fielder, who dove for the ball but missed it. "What do we have here, a bunch of babies, or are we going to be men?"

A short while later, I eavesdropped as the Hawks sat around Mr. Gardner. "Listen up! You look like a bunch of toddling babies out there, like a bunch of sissies. How are you going to win if every time a ball is hit a little too hard you jump out of the way? You've got to learn to take a couple of hard knocks. You've got to be tough to win, or you'll be losers all your life. Now, anybody got anything to say?"

One little hand went up. "Mr. Gardner, Dicky wet his pants again."

Mr. Gardner sneered down at Dicky, a three foot tot—only two feet sitting. "Why didn't you tell me you had to go to the bathroom?" he demanded.

Dicky whimpered, "You said in the last practice, no one was ever allowed to go to the bathroom again, Mr. Gardner, and if we did, we should do it in our pants." He then cried. His teammates empathized with him; they all stared sadly down at the dirt.

A coach must recognize his children's stage of development and capacities, or he will doom his little bright prospects to failure, just the opposite of his intent. If you met him on the street, you would think Mr. Gardner was a bit rough around the edges, but a well-meaning and very dedicated dad. He simply forgot that these children were not on the gridiron with the Raiders, but on the Little League diamond, being children. His expectations and those of his players were definitely not the same.

## I Cannot Believe I Said That!

Nothing saddens me more than hearing a parent or coach openly berate a Little Leaguer at bat. I cringe every time I hear one of the more benevolent coaches bellow out, "This one can't hit it," or "Hit it to second 'cause he can't catch."

Few adults realize how powerful their words truly are. We may think kids never listen, but certain words penetrate and are never forgotten. I learned this too late, in my second year as a T-ball manager.

One of the more talented children, Tammy, seemed depressed whenever I played with her. After the third practice, I put my arm over her shoulder and said, "What's wrong, Tammy?" She ignored me and walked away. Being well-versed in child psychiatry, though, I began to expertly probe, hoping I would hit a nerve that would open her up.

"I notice your dad isn't here. Does he play with you?"

"Sure," the girl said solemnly.

Tammy had not played with me last year, but I had noticed her talent and made sure to draft her in my second year as coach. This year, I had said to myself, I would have a first-place team! After a number of oblique psychological references, I saw I was not getting anywhere. I decided to try the honest approach.

"What's wrong, Tammy?"

She answered curtly, "You said I stunk last year, and I don't like you, I don't like baseball. My dad makes me play it."

I was shocked. Me? The great therapist had said this kid stunk? I later learned she had overheard me telling one of my players to hit the ball to a certain base, because that player could not catch. My Little Leaguer hit it to Tammy—and she remembered that a full year later. Had I unintentionally destroyed the confidence of a talented child? Just imagine what I had done to the confidence of the child I had really directed that comment to! Why, I asked myself, was I so insensitive to these little children, saying things like "He's no batter. Infield move in, he's an easy out." We coaches and parents must learn that our words can burn like a wildfire, or heal like a miracle. They wound the spirit of a child like a bullet, or instill confidence like a magical potion.

I started thinking back, remembering other remarks I had made without thinking. At one pre-game pep talk I had said, "Okay, kids, watch their infield—you see their third baseman has no arm."

Mary had yelled, "Yes, he does, Coach, he has two."

Another remark: "The second baseman can't catch."

"Yeah, I know," Carlos agreed. "He goes to school with me, and I already told him that. I will tell him you said so, too, Coach."

I think back on all the games I played with six- to twelve-year-olds in the past fourteen years. I long ago learned that winning or losing was not important to them as long as after the game I smiled and said, "You guys did a great job," and their parents hugged them and acted proud. I started doing this that second year, and we had a winning season pretty much from then on—despite the fact that I stopped recruiting talented kids and started looking, instead, for interested and loving parents. By the end of the season, no matter how many games we had lost, the children's faces would gleam, and their only sorrow would be that it was over until the next spring.

## Oh, Yes, They Hear Us

By the way, in case you ever wonder if your children are listening, let me tell you of a conversation I had with a fellow physician, my age, just the other day. We had been talking about children when I gently inquired why he and his wife had never had any. Thinking I would get the usual biological-problem explanation, I was stunned to hear it was due to his parents, who often spoke about him when he was well within earshot. What stood out most in his memory, he said, was his father's comment to several other coaches on the Little League field: "Sometimes I wish I had never had a son when I see how uncoordinated and goofy he looks out there." My friend was twelve at the time. From that moment on, he said, he decided not to have a child, because he did not want it to go through the same humiliation. I could not help but wonder if he was subconsciously afraid of humiliating his own son, or of his father doing it.

Please, parents, remember: children may not seem to be listening, but believe me, they hear every word, positive and negative, that we say about them. Every child wears an invisible sign that says NOTICE ME, MAKE ME FEEL IMPORTANT. Every time you look at the number of his or her uniform, see that sign!

# ten

## Children's Expectations

### *Happiness can be measured in smiles*

Greg looked like a modern version of Rodin's "Thinker" as his brow furrowed and his mighty chin rested on his hand. A scholarship to Arizona State, the 2002 Olympic team, a small jaunt at triple-A baseball, then right to the majors with a minimum of seven digits a season plus a healthy bonus. Ahhhh!!

Greg's son snapped him out of his daydream. "Gee, Dad, why can't I get one of those nifty green-and-yellow uniforms the A's have? When can I pick up the bat and hit the ball? Can we get a hamburger and fries after the game?"

Did you ever ask yourself what a child entering Little League for the first time thinks about playing baseball? What are his expectations? Most will answer, "I don't know," unless they have played with neighbors or their brothers or sisters. If you persist, they will say they want to have fun, which is exactly what adults initially say they want for their kids—that is, until they get indoctrinated by veteran parents and coaches to enter the world of competition and think about "winning." Competition means competing against others, trying to be better than your opponent— trying to beat him. Is that what a child really wants to do, compete and beat? Or does he want to play, like he did in preschool, and have fun with the other children? Play is the work of children —it is their job, the way they learn social skills.

This is a test. Do not panic. Just pick *A* or *B*.

A child of six, seven, or eight would rather:

1. (a) slide in the dirt
   (b) button his uniform and keep his hat on straight
2. (a) hit a ball and run
   (b) keep his shirt tucked in his pants
3. (a) have his parents cheer and smile at him
   (b) have his parents tell him to be quiet and listen

If you picked all *B*'s, you are a typical coach and average Little League parent. If you picked all *A*'s, you have a good sense of what children cherish and expect, and what Little League is all about. Surprised this chapter is so short? Children's expectations are short and simple—and make a lot of sense. Some of us should listen to them sometimes and have fun and play. It is obvious, isn't it?

# eleven

## "Winning Breeds Success"—or Does It?

*Winning is never final, losing is never fatal*

Not all coaches in Little League recognize the fallacy of "Winning breeds success," nor realize how possibly damaging it is to teach such an idea to children. Some coaches claim that winning is not everything, but what they really mean is "Winning is not a matter of life and death—it is much more than that!"

I had my own problems with the concept of winning during my first few years as a coach. Looking back, I am indeed horrified to recall how cruel and indifferent I was to such small children. Had I not known they had feelings? Certainly, I would never openly say to an adult the disparaging things I said to my players, even if they were true. He might punch me out or hold it against me. I was so competitive—talking about a "winning season." My T-ballers did not even know what that meant. Just imagine me announcing in the doctors' lounge, "Hey, fellas! My T-ball team is in first place! I'm something else, huh?" Yet, that was exactly what I was saying.

Then again, I like to think maybe it had not been my issue at all, but that of the parents who wanted their son or daughter on a "winning team." Had I been more influenced by what people thought than by what I believed was right? Had the problem been my expectations, or the expectations of the other parents?

I once heard a parent say, "Nothing breeds success like winning." If this is true, then at least 50 percent of all T-ballers will learn to be failures at six years of age, since only one team wins the game. In fact, over a season, if there are five or six teams and only one can come in first, 80 percent of the league's children will be failures! Now, whose expectations will that satisfy?

Even now, in my mind's eye, I can see my dad's expression of disappointment whenever my team lost. Maybe I had still been trying to make my dad happy, still trying to make up for my high-school baseball team being 79 and 1 (seventy-nine losses, one win) during my four years there. Could it possibly have been that my ego was on the line, and the children enjoying themselves came second?

We adults can and must learn to put our own expectations second, and our children's needs and enjoyment first. This is easier to do with conscious expectations, of course, but finding out what your unconscious expectations are is not difficult—they are often apparent to the people around you. All you have to do is listen, or ask!

## Dominic and Charlie

The batter, not much taller than the bat he was swinging, hit the ball to the second baseman and dashed to first base. On second base, Dominic knocked the ball down, then picked it up and threw it over the first baseman's head. The coach yelled angrily, "What are you doing, sleeping? Never throw the ball when you can't get them out." He then turned and kicked the fence in disgust. Dominic's eyes filled with tears, his little body trembled. His teammates tensed up, hoping the next ball would not be hit to them.

On another diamond that same day, a ball was hit to Charlie, who also knocked it down and picked it up. He, too, threw the ball over the first baseman's head. His coach yelled, "Great stop, Charlie, that's getting in front of it, nice arm."

Charlie's smile reflected that of his coach. The rest of the parents chimed in, "Nice stop, Charlie."

On this team, the coach realized what was most important for a child at this age: effort. The rest of the team could not wait until a ball was hit to them. The positive remark had allowed Charlie to see the good he had done, which encouraged him to go after the ball again. Dominic, on the other hand, was worrying about his throw even before he caught the next ball. Once again, encouragement sparked effort, the first ingredient of success. Yes, effort, not winning, breeds success. Continued effort, in time, breeds discipline. Children can develop these traits whether they are talented or not—it all depends on you, their coach.

## Substitute Parents

A recent survey noted that the most successful children were not the ones with the highest IQ's or the greatest motor skills, but those who felt their parents never gave up on them. A child who knows his parents are always supportive feels safe and content. He brings these feelings into the rest of his life. Do you really think he will remember at twenty-five how he mishandled a fly ball when he was seven? Well, I suppose he could—if you made it painful enough for him, and constantly reminded him of his "error." As a coach, you are a parental substitute; your positive reinforcement is as important as a mom's or dad's praise.

Children often judge whether an experience is positive by the way the adults in their lives react. You must see and express the positive in every strike, dropped ball, and bad call. Yes, even accentuate the positive about the opposing team, their coach, and the umpire. In my first parent-coach meeting of each year, I would instruct the parents to display unconditional positive regard for every child on the team, and every person on or connected to the field. Remarks like "He stinks, the umpire is blind," and, especially, "My child's better than——," were not tolerated. "Nice play," "Good catch," "Great swing," "Good try" are the words of unconditional positive regard.

In my seventh year, I learned that writing up large posters with NICE PLAY, GREAT HIT, and GOOD TRY were a way of maintaining this positive regard and spirit of the team. When one of the children made a good effort, the NICE PLAY sign would go up to the cheers of the parents. The smiles on the children's faces made the sun pale in comparison at times.

# twelve

## Positive Against All Odds

### *Children must believe to achieve*

A fundamental principle in Little League is being positive. While this may seem a little too fundamental to bother stating, when you truly look at baseball you realize being positive is no simple task.

First, one team always loses.

Second, twenty-one outs have to be made among nine players.

Third, there will be at least three errors for each out made in T-ball. In the farm system, you can expect one error to every out. Even in the minors, the players average one error to every two outs at the beginning of the season.

To complicate matters, the umpire is usually a parent or a high-school student, twelve to fifteen years of age, who often will please no one with his or her refereeing. As one can imagine, baseball is a regular paradise for anyone looking to belittle others. Frustrated parents too intimidated to yell at their bosses and spouses also find it a great outlet. Here they can attack the umpires, berate the managers and coaches, and demean all the players on the field with impunity. Some go the full hundred yards in criticizing their children's own teammates—and even their own children:

"How much did they pay you, ump?"

"Where did you learn how to play baseball?"

"My son never was any good at sports—or school."

"Johnny stinks, get him out of the infield."

"Why is he playing first base? We will never win with him there."

Yes, these cruel and demeaning remarks are said right in front of the children. And, yes, baseball is filled with errors, misjudgments, miscalls, and mistakes. Just imagine your child getting 67 percent of all his test questions in school wrong, and only 33 percent correct. Well, in baseball, if he gets on base once for every three times at bat, he is considered a very good batter.

## First, the Tony Principle

The first rule of being positive is to eliminate the negative. That reminds me of a play I will never forget.

Tony, a very enthusiastic and energetic Little Leaguer, was on the pitcher's mound. *Clank!* The ball, hit off the tee, went straight to him. It bounced into his glove, and bounced right out. Error number one.

Tony quickly picked the ball up and threw it fiercely to first base. Instead of going toward the first baseman's glove, though, the ball hit the corner of the bag, causing it to bounce right back toward Tony. Error number two.

As he ran to pick it up, Tony took his eye off the ball to look at the runner. The ball went right through his legs. Error number three.

Tony turned around to retrieve the ball that was now sitting on the pitcher's mound and threw it toward second base. A perfect throw—if the second baseman had been King Kong, twenty feet tall. Error number four.

The ball bounced out into center field. The center fielder finally retrieved it, and tossed it home just as the batter rounded third base and headed for the plate. Yes, Tony, in his enthusiasm, was right there blocking off his own catcher on home plate. The ball rolled into home—in and out of Tony's shiny glove once again. Error number five.

Unbelievable? Absolutely! Did it really happen? Oh, yes! The American Major League record for errors from one player is three in one inning, but whatever the major leaguers can do, Little

Leaguers can do better. So how did I react to this incredible performance of five errors in one play by the same player? Phenomenal! I was hoarse from screaming, delirious from all the commotion. "What effort, what enthusiasm! I am sure that one play could go into the *Guinness Book of Records!*" I, and everyone else, marveled at Tony's effort, and cheered our heads off. Tony, well, he smiled, shrugged his shoulders, and enthusiastically awaited the next batter.

Sure, I could have made any number of negative remarks—the list that comes readily to mind is almost endless. I could have benched him for the rest of the season; I could have burned his glove, put him on waivers. That would certainly have made the play into a disaster Tony would never forget. Would it have made the game more fun? Would it have made Tony feel better? Would it have been a good, growth experience? The answers are obvious.

You can always find the positive if you look hard enough. We cheered Tony's effort, we cheered his enthusiasm, we cheered his energy and alertness. A few years later, Tony was elected to the all-stars team for three years in a row. Did he remember making five errors in one play? No!

## Beyond Simple "Errors"

Then there was Freddy. Freddy was on second base; no one was on first. "Yo, Freddy, remember: if the ball is hit to third, you do not have to run to third," I, the third-base coach, called to him. Freddy gave me a confident thumbs-up sign; he had heard and understood what I said. Freddy also remembered that in the last game, he had run to third base and gotten tagged out. *Whack!* The ball was hit to third. I quickly glanced to see if Freddy was coming. Thank God he was not.

Oh, no—Freddy was running to first! He got there safe.

"What a slide," I yelled to him as he was called out. "Freddy, good listening. I am proud you did not go to third, just like I told you. That slide was great. After the game, we will go over running the bases again." I said all this with a big grin. Luckily, I was in my seventh year of coaching by then. If this had happened during my first, my response might have been dramatically different, possibly causing a bleeding ulcer for one of us, and a brain hemorrhage for the other. Unharmed, Freddy continued to play and often was the first child at practice.

Kirit was at third base. "Yo, Kirit! Remember, you have to tag the runner if the ball is thrown to you. Stepping on the bag is not enough."

"Got it, Coach. Tag." *Boom!* The ball was hit to the pitcher. The man from second, disregarding his coach's pleas to stay there, was off in full gear toward third. Kirit, catching the ball from the pitcher, was standing in front of the bag. The collision was inevitable. But, no, Kirit jumped out of the way and let the opponent arrive safely at third base—then he tagged him with the ball.

I yelled, "Great catch from the pitcher, Kirit, and great tag. Next time, let's tag him before he reaches the bag."

"Okay, Coach." Kirit smiled, content with himself. The positive is always there; sometimes, in Little League, you just need a little creative thinking to find it.

Ron, a lanky, awkward child, was at bat. The ball was on the tee. He positioned his bat right on it, as I had taught him. He brought the bat back to the ready position and swung with all the first-grade muscles he could muster. The tee landed about two feet in front of the plate. "Great swing, Ron."

The umpire set up the tee again. I hollered instructions: "Keep your eye on the ball."

Ron riveted his eyes on the ball and swung. He missed everything. "That's keeping your eye on the ball," I said. The ball was set up again. He swung and missed. After ten times, the infield began to get restless. The second baseman was building a dirt mound. The outfield, distracted by cheers from the majors in the opposite field, was, consequently, facing the wrong direction altogether.

"Those are good practice swings, Ron. Now, show them how far you can hit the ball." After two more swings, Ron hit a nice drive just past third base. He arrived on first base with a big smile. Later, I am told, he said to the first-base coach, "I didn't realize I was practicing until the coach reminded me."

Yes, the creative genius is there in all of us—it just takes an
opportunity like Little League to bring it out. As a coach or manager in Little League, your creativity will be tested to its limits.
Eliminate the negative, accentuate the positive, always be affirmative, and remember: children need our support most when
they seem to deserve it least.

## Andy's Story

Andy was a slightly built, gentle little fellow. His dad had decided he should forgo Little League after his first two years were
spent playing the bench. Mr. Clemmon was discouraged because,
despite all efforts, Andy never seemed to progress farther than
the dugout. He felt Andy's lack of physical stature would probably doom him to continual failure, making the Little League experience less than beneficial, to say the least. After listening to Mr.
Clemmon talk about the boy's plight, I persuaded him to have
Andy play for me. Why? I guess because I love an underdog—he
reminds me of me!

Initially, it appeared that Andy's dad was dead right. Everything
the child did seemed a chore to him. His throw was not hard
enough to break a window pane, even if he could make a direct
hit; his swing was so slow, a spider could have spun a full web
before he connected—or missed—the ball. One day, out of des-
perate inspiration, I told Andy he was one of the fastest base
runners on the team. Suddenly, his face changed—his whole body
seemed to straighten out a little more. Hey, I thought, give him a
pat on the back, and behind this thin little figure stands one determined young man.

After learning the basics and gaining a modicum of confidence,
Andy decided he wanted to be, of all things, the catcher. Yes, the
catcher—the guy who stood where the would-be football or
hockey players get to be. You know, the guy who stands there in
front of home plate just daring you to cross their path. I tried to
counsel Andrew, but his heart was set. I decided to give him the
chance—besides, his parents had already bought him a catcher's
glove.

As he crouched behind the plate, our pitcher, Tony, threw fireballs to him. Andy's eyes watered from the force; after several innings, he gingerly removed his glove from his hand as one takes off a Band-Aid from a wound. I asked if he would like to play another position, but he answered unequivocally, "No. I can do it."

As time went on, this child, who could barely swing a bat, became one of the best catchers in the league, and by far the best base runner. His secret, no doubt, was his parents and older brother, who gave him unconditional support and praise. My part had just been to give him the atmosphere to grow, and the feeling that someone believed in him. Andrew played with more than his body for me—he played with all his heart.

# Section Three

---

# HARMONY
# AMID DISCORD

*Spend less time concerned with who is right
and more time deciding what is right*

Some things in life simply are not taught in grammar school, high school, or college. They must be learned through life experience. Little League, too, has ingredients that cannot be found in books, nor in the usual baseball camp. Focusing, consistency, and harmony must be learned on the diamond with the bleachers full, the sun blazing, and the parents, coaches, and young players interacting.

# thirteen

## Focus

### *Keeping the attention of the MTV generation*

Major leaguers always talk about focus—focusing their eye on the ball, focusing their attention on the play, focusing their energy. With proper focus, the pros claim, one can anticipate every potential eventuality, make the correct choice without hesitation, and predict and outsmart one's opponents. Orel Hershiser, Tommy John, Mickey Mantle, Willie Mays, and Brett Butler all focused and made things happen. The great managers, such as Tommy Lasorda, seem to be born with focus.

In Little League T-ball, farm, minors, and even majors, focus primarily comes down to paying attention. If a first-time coach does not know the average attention span of a six-to-twelve-year-old child—or if he expects to have a field of Babe Ruths, Ty Cobbs, Mike Piazzas, Tom Seavers, and Jim Palmers—he is in for unexpected hair loss (from pulling it out in frustration), headaches (from slamming the palm of his hand into his forehead in disbelief), and upset stomachs (from jumping up and down in mini-tantrums). I am sure you have seen this coach before. He is the rookie—and Little League goes through many rookie coaches. Fifty percent of all coaches do not return the following year, a statistic rarely quoted in the league. The ones who do return either have given in to the guilt piled on by their league presidents and vice presidents or have learned the trick of keeping their sanity: keep the team alert and focused.

Sixth inning of the crucial game. The score was . . . well, being the kind of manager who was more concerned with my ballplayers, I did not care about the score, but if the Hawks managed to make four more runs, my hopes of a first-place team would fade into the horizon.

José was up for the Hawks. The ball, sitting innocently on the tee, was just two feet from him. He swung and missed five times in a row. The only safe place for the ball was on the tee! My pitcher, Alan, raised his hand as soon as he saw I wasn't looking, and yelled, "Coach, I have to go to the bathroom." Just at that moment, José swung for the sixth time and, wonder of wonders, hit the ball to second base. An easy grounder—if Brent had not been lying down with his head nicely propped up by his glove, that is. The ball rolled to the outfield. I screamed, "Danny, get in front of it!" Danny, however, had nodded off. My shout jolted him momentarily to reality, but he had no idea where the ball was.

"Did it pass me? Is it in front of me? Where am I?"

Suddenly, Danny saw the ball lying next to him. He picked it up and tossed it to left field, where Amy was watching the dandelions grow. At the last moment, she raised her hand and caught the ball on the fly. She held up the shiny white sphere for all of us to admire, and proudly yelled, "He's out. I caught the ball on a fly."

In the meantime, Mr. Sane Coach was having a mini-tantrum. I was jumping up and down screaming, "Throw the ball, throw the ball, throw the ball home!" José was skipping around second and going toward third. By now, all the players had gotten the message and were on alert. Amy, however, was not aware that the ball had been thrown, rather than hit, to her, and would not give it up. José crossed the plate to the howling of the opposing crowd. I had bruises on both thighs from hitting myself, a sore throat from screaming, and had made an utter fool of myself in front of all the parents to boot.

To save face, if not your sanity, the next time you find yourself in a similar situation, you might take note of some facts I have acquired since then.

First, the average attention span of a six-year-old in the outfield is four to six minutes. A seven-year-old with one year of experience can last five to seven minutes, and an eight-year-old with two years' experience might make it ten to fifteen minutes. A nine-year-old with experience is good for ten to fifteen minutes, while a child ten or older should be able to stay focused for fifteen to twenty minutes. Take off one minute in each category for players with no experience. In T-ball, take off another minute for each inning played.

What all this means is that a child of six can be expected to pay attention for no more than two to three minutes in the third inning of a T-ball game. In other words, if your T-ball team is all first-year rookies, they will be "gone" by the time they reach their positions in the outfield and turn to face home plate. In fact, I once had a player go all the way to the snack bar three hundred yards away before he realized he was supposed to stop in center field. You, as the coach, must do something to refocus them—that is, if you haven't already nodded off yourself.

Coaching T-ball is not an easy job, nor one for someone who is not ready to use his lungs for something other than breathing.

## Cheer Them On

You could have fried an egg on home plate as the sun blazed down on Pasadena Little League Field at Hamilton Park. The ballplayers looked like they would gladly run in if anyone suggested it was nap time. They would probably have even run to the dugout to do homework, just to get out of the sun. Top of the third inning. The first batter up for the Giants hadn't yet gotten to the batter's box, but Chris, on third base, had already squatted down like an Indian ready to pass around the peace pipe. Not ten seconds later, all the outfielders joined him. I bellowed, "Who are we?"

Several feeble, squeaky voices said, "Da Padres."

I hollered again, "Who are we?"

Now added to the voices of the several were the distant calls of the outfielders. "The Padres."

I shouted one more time, "Who?"

With moderate gusto, they whooped, "The Padres!"

"Are we ready?"

At that, the team was awake. In unison, they yelled, "Ready!"

"Ready positions," I called with authority. They jumped to their "gorilla" position, arms hanging from their shoulders to the ground and swaying gently back and forth. My team was focused . . . for a while.

The outfielders were all first-year rookies, so they were good for four to six minutes, less one minute for each inning and two minutes for severe environmental (heat) factors. That made five minutes off their optimum six-minute attention span, which meant they needed to be refocused every few minutes. In a situation like this, I could only hope they would continue to face home plate—some do not. The best way I found to combat the doldrums and keep their attention was the series of cheers—"Who are we? Are we ready? Do we ever give up?"—that I used throughout my twelve-year career as a coach and manager. They were so effective that by my second year, other coaches began using them and making up more of their own.

Do not worry about your team getting tired of doing the same few cheers over and over. Young children love monotony; they can hear the same story endlessly ("Dad, tell me again about the Three Little Pigs"). Remember, repetition makes memory. In Little League, above all it focuses attention, which is what prevents some child from being hit by a ball because he or she got distracted; it even gives the players an opportunity to make a catch.

## Just When I Had Their Attention

The fifth and probably final inning. I stood at the entrance to the dugout, a baseball in one hand and a bat in the other. We had played a long but fruitful game and were down by only two runs. The real problem, however, was that my Little Leaguers were fading quickly, like a red chameleon on a green leaf. I had to refocus them. I called them to gather round, but my series of "Who are we?" cheers had little effect. Looking at their tired faces, I tried my next trick: "Who would you rather be—the ball or the bat?" I stretched both out to them. Several yelled, "The bat!"

"Yes," I said with enthusiasm, "because the bat always clobbers the ball!" They liked this, as usual. I gently sent the ball flying off the bat. "Who has the bat now?" I queried mischievously.

"We do," several answered.

"Who?"

"We do!" they all chimed.

"*Who* has the . . ."

Before I could finish, Sean yelled, "Look, there's a frog!" All heads turned away from me suddenly, but no one moved until the magical word was spoken: "It's a bullfrog!"

With that, I found myself like a mime, frozen with arms outstretched and vivid with expression—standing alone. All my Little Leaguers abandoned ship to chase the bullfrog. Did I feel bad, ignored, in doubt about my sense of leadership or ability to instill enthusiasm and focus my team? You bet I did. I had lost their attention—but I did not lose the lesson. Next time, I'll use going to the zoo as a motivator!

## Cheer the Parents

Cheering works just as well with parents as with children, and is a nice way to break up your own feelings of monotony. As I would notice the dads and moms drifting off into mundane and boring conversations, or getting the too-many-hot-dogs-before-the-game nods, I would yell, "Do our children ever give up?"

"No," they would holler in return.

Then: "Who are we?"

"Padre Parents!"

"Who?"

"Padre Parents!"

"Louder!"

"*Padre Parents!*"

I would most often lead the parents in cheers when our team was down or having a hard time focusing despite their cheers. Somehow, when the dads and moms cheered, it inspired the boys and girls on the field. Everyone gets inspired when they hear their family root for them. I have heard professional players say, "This one is for you, Mom," or an announcer remark, "Orel's parents are in the park today." Somehow, having your folks in the stands lends an air of mystique—everyone knows that a professional ballplayer will be so much "more" for that particular game because his mom and dad are in the stands. I do not know if a study has ever been done to see if parents' presence makes a difference in professional baseball, but my statistics definitely prove they count in Little League. Give me a stand full of parents, and I will give you a field full of contented, focused Little Leaguers. Get the picture?

# fourteen

## Consistency: Secret for Parental Success

### *Children do as you do, not as you say*

Consistency, in the American and National Leagues, means reliability. A "golden glover" will rarely make an error; a .300 hitter with a .450 batting average can be counted on to bring home the runners who are in scoring position, no matter what. In professional baseball, consistency refers to a person who, when the pressure is on, always rises to the occasion. Practice is probably one of the main ingredients for developing that consistency, but I will bet there is an additional element, one that instills the self-discipline to practice: consistent, supportive parents. Self-discipline in children does not come automatically or overnight, but is bred by their parents. In Little League, then, consistency really refers to reliable parents.

Several interesting studies have shown that children grow up feeling more secure when they have consistent parents. Consistent does not necessarily mean strict discipline; it means that regardless of whether the parents are strict, somewhat liberal, or in-between, they are consistently that way. (The extremes of neglect and smothering were, of course, found to be harmful.) Parents who respond to problems and situations in a like manner all the time make their child feel secure. The child does not need to agree with them; he only has to know he can count on their sensible response. Another major factor in a child's sense of security, the study noted, is having both parents respond in a similar manner and agree on what is significant, or important. Continual conflicts between parents cause confusion and is often a sign of a shaky marriage, something children can sense, even when the yelling, finger wagging, and arguments occur in supposed secrecy. Some children get frightened by their parents' conflicts; some find ways to use it to their advantage. Either way, they learn some disturbing lessons from our inconsistent ways.

## The Old Divide and Conquer

As I stood in front of the stands, chubby-cheeked Mario went up to his mom. "Mommy, can I have some money for a hot dog and nacho chips 'n cheese?"

"No, Mario," she answered seriously, "I have a nice, nutritious lunch ready for you at home for after the game. Remember our talk about good food and losing some weight?"

Mario's cherub face frowned and his head drooped. *Aw, but, Mom!*

About fifteen minutes later, after the game, I stood in line at the snack bar—ready to order carrot sticks and yogurt, of course, to go along with my hot dog. In front of me I heard a familiar voice. "Gee, thanks, Dad."

"Two hot dogs with nacho chips and extra cheese and a Coke, please," Mario said. His dad bent over to talk into Mario's ear.

"Now, don't tell Mom."

"Don't worry, Dad, your secret's mine."

I wondered if Mario's dad did this often. Maybe that was why Mario always found a way out of running the bags, was always the last one on the field, and generally did the least he could to get by—and he was only eight.

## Open Warfare

When George managed, he was obviously the boss, the one wearing the pants, the one calling the shots—that is, until Cheryl, his wife, would arrive in the stands. A big man at 250 pounds, George seemed to grow a deeper red as each of his orders to his ballplayers was second-guessed by his wife. Their son, Jeff, would sag lower and lower as the game progressed, obviously embarrassed.

Whenever Cheryl contradicted George, he would tell her to shut up and go to——. She would respond with similar expletives —yes, right there in the middle of the ball field. The first time I heard them, I almost expected to see *Roseanne* sprouting from some portable television. Some of George and Cheryl's exchanges were quite inventive and funny. If you listened long enough, though, you realized they meant what they were saying to each other. Many of the parents, including me, felt very uneasy as their interchanges grew progressively nastier. Jeff would simply try to disappear. Then it happened.

It was a Sunday afternoon. George's team, the Twins, had just lost their third close game in a row, this time on a squeeze play he had called, but which had backfired. As the Twins shuffled to the dugout for the final "2-4-6-8" cheer, Cheryl yelled out, "Well, you blew another game, you idiot! I hope you're . . ."

Before she could finish, George spun around and roared, "That's it! I'm quitting! I'm quitting Little League, and I'm quitting this marriage!" Well, those were not his words exactly . . . but the sentiment, sans expletives, is the same. What happened to Jeff? I do not know. He never showed up again on any Little League team I know of—he probably spent the rest of his childhood trying to fade into the woodwork, just as he had spent his Little League career trying to fade into the outfield.

## Inconsistency, Indecision

Chad stood on second base. As the ball was hit, he took five or six quick steps toward third, then froze. The third-base coach yelled, "Run, run!" You could see the indecision on Chad's face as he bit his lower lip and anxiously looked around. The shortstop came running up with the ball in his hand. As he reached out to make the tag, Chad began to run, but it was too late. Chad started to cry and stomp his feet in frustration. He tore his hat from his head and walked toward the dugout, his chin down nearly to his belly.

This behavior was not unusual for Chad. Anyone who knew his parents knew why he was this way. If I asked them to be at a specific practice, they would hem and haw, finally say yes, and then not show up—or, even stranger, they would say they could not make it, and then come. They often dropped Chad off late; sometimes, he did not get to practice at all. Frequently he did not have his equipment and had to borrow other children's. His parents were rarely at the games; if someone did show up, it was always one or the other, never both. On more than one occasion, either his mom or dad would arrive before the game ended and pull him out to go home; they would flatly state he had been playing long enough. I never knew what to expect from them—and neither did Chad.

Children who are brought up without consistency, like Mario, Jeff, and Chad, become confused, chronically anxious, and frustrated. They never know when the other shoe will fall. They take on their parents' uncertainty and turn timid. Their reaction to their environment becomes inconsistent and a source of frustration. They develop into what all parents hope their children will not be: a child who is insecure, indecisive, and frightened. When they are under pressure, they do not have the inner security needed to see them through the rough spots in life.

What can help children like this? What do they lack? Harmony. Harmony comes when a child's environment is healthy, safe, consistent, and predictable; when he can count on and trust the behavior of parents, teachers, and coaches; when his parents support each other. Harmony is the element that will allow your child's natural abilities and talents to flourish.

# fifteen

## Overcoming "Natural" Instincts

*Children may be children, but parents should be more*

I had just sat down and turned on the TV. With my remote control, I swiftly raced through the channels until I hit a ball game. As the pitcher threw the ball, the batter dove out of the way to avoid being hit. In a flash, the batter raced to the mound with flailing fists. Before he could do any damage, though, he was tackled by the third baseman. Both dugouts emptied. Soon, I could not distinguish one team from the other; the players seemed to meld into a chaotic mass that ebbed and flowed with grunts, groans, and a mixture of unintelligible words. The broadcaster excitedly recounted each blow. Was this baseball? Where did all those guys go, who used to stand with their hats over their hearts as "The Star Spangled Banner" was belted out by the soprano?

Harmony is the opposite of such chaos; it is order and teamwork in an atmosphere of mutual respect. Some team sports, like football, maintain a delicate balance between harmony and chaos. One moment everything is symmetrical and orderly; the next moment, the field is filled with mayhem and twisted bodies. Baseball, of course, is (supposedly) more civilized. At times, though, something takes over that destroys the order and camaraderie. Did you ever wonder which comes more naturally to human nature, harmony or chaos?

History demonstrates that survival of the fittest, and the establishment of boundaries and pecking orders, is "natural." Children, especially, quickly determine who is the toughest in the class, who is the prettiest, who is the best, who is the fastest. Unfortunately, the other side of the coin is fixing who is the ugliest, the slowest, the worst. Children effortlessly decide who is "in" and who is "out"; who is rad or cool, and who is a nerd. We, as adults, know this is immature, and it makes us angry. We shake our heads over how children can be so cruel to one another. Yet, when you think about our own "grown-up" behavior, is it all that different?

Take a look at this exchange:

"Hi, my name is Leon. Nice to meet you, Kevin." Leon and Kevin shake hands. In ancient years, handshaking was a way of making sure your adversary did not have a weapon. Now, it is a ritual of manliness; Leon shakes Kevin's hand firmly and decisively. "Which child is yours, Kevin?"

Kevin points to his son, who towers over all the other children.

"He's a big boy," Leon says in a surprised voice.

"Yeah, he gets it from his mother's side. Her brothers are all six-five or more. Which one is yours?"

"Jeremy, over there, is my son."

Kevin's son towers over Leon's boy by a head. Leon now feels a little intimidated, especially after noticing that Kevin's son is as talented as he is big. After a little while, he asks Kevin, "Do you live nearby?"

"Yes, over there near Poor Pines Road."

"Oh, on Poor Pines Road? I live up the hill, in Big Bucks Manor. What do you do for a living, Kevin?"

"I'm a carpenter."

Kevin recognizes the game, so does not bother to ask Leon what he does. Still feeling somewhat inferior, though, or maybe just irritated because he let himself feel that way at first, Leon tells him just the same.

"I work for the Sue Them All firm as a lawyer. That's spelled *a-t-t-o-r-n-e-y*."

This conversation, of course, is a complete fabrication. I'm sure none of us has ever met anyone so crude, because, as adults, we are above these kinds of childish status games, are we not? Our sophistication and hard-won wisdom have taught us to abandon such puerile comments as "I am the toughest," "I am the best," or "I am the prettiest." All we care about is who has the biggest house, the best car, the best job, and the most money.

Interestingly, the first question most adults want to ask of an individual they do not know is not their name, but what they do, what their job is. In other words, what is their status? Asking about someone's occupation is the adult way of finding out who is the toughest, who is the best.

Yes, most of us really are still children. We are simply more adept at disguising our basic competitive traits, which, if left unbridled, can become destructive and chaotic. Fortunately, we developed other attributes as we grew to adulthood that counteract our fundamental chaotic tendencies. We have acquired compassion, generosity, and empathy, the hallmarks of civilized society. These are the qualities we hope to instill in our children, the virtues all parents wish for their children. They make us feel sorry for those who are less fortunate, ill, in danger, or in need of help. They are not easy to impart, though—especially in Little League, where, some would have you believe, the entire purpose of the game is to beat your opponent.

How can we, as parents and coaches, teach our children harmony and provide for them the kind of safe, trusting environment that will start them out on the road toward being good, moral, and wholesome people? First, we must teach it to ourselves and each other.

# sixteen

# Teaching Children Harmony

*Little League is a song*
*The bat leads the beat*
*The ball carries the tune*
*The cheers are the choir*
*—Coach Fortanasce*

Children flourish when they feel safe. They look to us for safety, security, and protection—at times, even from one another. After all, Little Leaguers can get hurt in plenty of ways other than by being hit by a ball or called out on a strike. Words and actions can leave invisible scars that create defenses within and shape negative reactions for life. These kinds of words and actions happen when a Little League coach does not make harmony—teamwork, order, safety, mutual respect—the most important part of the game.

## Children Will Be Children

Everett could only be described as awkward, thin, and lanky. It seemed, at times, that his left foot loved to step on his right. His brown locks were always in disarray, and his nose, like Jimmy Durante's, seemed to eclipse his tiny mouth and soft brown eyes.

He was gentle and shy—just the kind of child to make everyone else feel he was different.

Don was a talented Little Leaguer, but as young as he was, he could be as demeaning and cruel as any adult. He was the kid we all feared in our own childhoods—the proverbial bully, the one who got his self-worth from pushing others around. The object of his contempt today was, as usual, Everett.

The Yankees coach hit the ball to Everett. It went into his glove, up his arm, into his chin, and landed on the ground in front of him. A demeaning giggle came from Don. "You stink, Everett. You really stink."

"Good thing it didn't hit you in the nose," chimed in Ky, "or it might have got stuck up there." That brought titters from everyone.

"Hey, anteater-nose, you don't need no bat, just swing your nose. You're bound to get a hit." This brought a greater roar.

Children learn destructive behavior so quickly. All they need is an instigator. When the team came off the field, the onslaught continued. Don took Everett's hat, bent it, put it on his nose, and walked around the dugout bumping into everyone, mimicking Everett's awkward walk. Some of the other children poked Everett, who could only frown and try his best to hold in his tears.

"Hey, Don, give Everett his nose back—I mean his hat," said the coach as he smiled and chuckled. "And stop picking on him," he added halfheartedly. As soon as he turned around, though, one of the other children grabbed Everett's hat again and started swatting him with it.

Soon, the mischievous bunch turned their attention to picking on "Chubs," as they had nicknamed Bobby. Don took Everett's hat and bumped into Richie, who threw out his belly to mimic "Chubs." The other children laughed at the two boys.

Bobby began to cry, which was, of course, the signal for all the little men to chime in with a chorus of "Cry, baby, cry. Stick your finger in your eye. Tell your mother it wasn't I. Cry, baby, cry." More than simply the words, it was the children's whining, demeaning tone that hurt Bobby and deprived him of any respect for himself. Yes, Bobby was learning peer pressure. His mom and dad had never done this to him. They loved and respected him. Now his friends were telling him he was not acceptable because he was fat. To a child, being "not acceptable" is the same thing as being bad, or rejected. Seven years after this incident—and many more like it, unfortunately—Bobby told me, "I cannot trust people anymore. They will hurt me."

Did he remember where he learned this? Oh, yes. Not surprisingly, Bobby does not like team sports today. Bobby and Everett blame the other players for what happened to them. When Everett's parents complained to the coach, he pulled out the old, worn, "Well, children will be children!" There was nothing, he claimed, he could—or should—have done to stop them. "You can't control them. Kids have to fend for themselves. That is how they learn to grow up."

Separation anxiety, the fear of being left alone, is a child's first and greatest dread. Children feel safe when an adult is around. They bloom with firm, loving control. When left alone—physically or emotionally—they, like adults, compete to stay in the "in" crowd, even if they do not like the people in it, just so they will not be by themselves. Remember, though, to be in the "in" crowd, someone must be in the "out" crowd. After all, how would you know who is "in" if you did not know who is "out"?

A coach does not—and should not—have to tolerate the kind of behavior that made Bobby's and Everett's Little League careers so miserable. Children do not have to be permitted to "do what comes naturally," to be cruel. They can be stopped, and guided to a safer, more harmonic road—but only if someone is there to teach a higher level of civilization than dog-eat-dog. Never accept the unacceptable.

## Coaches and Parents in Harmony

Have you ever wondered where bullies—the children who throw their weight around, the ones whose tone can hurt much more than a fist—come from? Some parents like to think they learn these behaviors on their own, or from their friends, but they do not. They learn them at home.

It never ceases to amaze me how much children mimic their parents in all ways, including the expletives and four-letter words they hear Dad and Mom use—not *base*, *ball*, and *bats*, but the *F* word and the *S* word. These are damaging, not harmonious, words. They hurt the people they are used against—and they hurt the people who have gotten into the habit of using them.

"Damn it, Mark. You can't hit a barn with a bat!"

Mark had missed the ball sitting on the tee, but this was not his coach or his dad talking; it was Mark himself. He was seven years old. His hat was crooked sideways. He stood just a little taller than the tee. He stopped trying to hit the ball, and started kicking the tee as he yelled, "Shit, shit!"

I remembered hearing Mark's dad make the exact same remark just two days earlier: "Damn, you can't hit a barn with a bat." Obviously Mark had added the other expletive on his own—but, of course, he must have learned that at school!

As coach, you can and must set the stage for the parents. Just because they have jobs and have produced children does not necessarily mean they ever grew up. Listen to them and the other coaches at your next Little League game. If you close your eyes, it will be hard to distinguish the children from the adults by their conversation. You can—and must—establish what words and behavior you will and will not tolerate from your team's parents. Make your point at the first meeting, then make it again just before the first game, and then again at every game after that, if necessary.

At my first parent-coach meeting of every season, I would explain in no uncertain terms that the words and behavior adults used at Little League games were extremely important and powerful tools—tools the children would copy. What was said and how the children were treated by the team parents would influence not only how those children treated their friends, but also how they would treat Mom and Dad later in life, when the roles of who-is-supporting-whom became reversed. All the parents had to agree:

1. Never to laugh at or criticize a child for something they, as adults, might consider an error.
2. Never to curse or criticize a child in front of the child's friends. Talk to them after the game, or talk to the coach. Exceptions, of course, included correcting a child who was doing something dangerous, such as swinging a bat.
3. Never to openly criticize the umpire, another coach, or someone else's child.

When a coach or manager establishes these criteria, he creates a harmonious atmosphere that fosters teamwork and mutual respect. In such an environment, children also learn respect for authority—and remember, umpires are the authority in Little League. Demeaning them ("Hey, ump, what are you, blind?") gives a strong message to little people. Open criticism of coaches and other players in front of the children is also ill-advised, and often potentially destructive. A one-on-one confrontation, or a discussion with the league president or vice president, is the best way to air any complaints about a coach's, manager's, or umpire's wrong or inappropriate conduct. If you do talk to the umpire or coach, always do it in private. (The one time any parent must stand up publicly to a coach or manager, however, is when that person is being destructive to a child. Making sure the children feel protected comes before everything else.) If you wonder if you are making the correct decision, ask the other parents if their perception of the situation is the same. Then act.

Children also need to see that you, the parent or the coach, respect authority. They learn how to deal with life's inevitable conflicts from watching you. You can teach them to treat their adversaries with honesty and respect, or with derision and destructiveness. Don't forget, though, that if you choose the latter, you will be teaching your child rudeness and unruliness, and will eventually bear the fruits of those teachings yourself, when your children reach their teenage years. You will have taught them how to deal with you!

## Someone Is in Control

Miguel giggled and yelled, "You stink!" as Lewis missed the ball on the tee for the third time in the practice. Giggling and making fun of someone else is infectious to T-ballers; several of the other children began to laugh, too.

Suddenly, the coach bellowed, "Who said, 'You stink'? Speak up! You think laughing at someone is funny? Well, I think it is not very nice. I never want to hear or see anything like this again! Miguel, tell Lewis you are sorry, immediately."

Miguel looked up defiantly and said, "No."

The coach marched right over to Miguel and sat him on the bench. He then turned to the rest of the players and told them that anyone who laughed at another teammate for missing a ball, or any other reason, would be off the team.

The little boys had never seen their coach like this. He was always smiling; he always spoke in an enthusiastic tone. Were they afraid? No. There was no fear on their faces. Quite the contrary—they looked calm. Someone was in control—someone who would prevent them from getting hurt, who would allow only praise and good comments from and for one another, and who would protect them from being laughed at by the others. Children flourish when they feel safe. They look to us parents and coaches for this protection, this peace. They expect it—and they deserve it.

Remember Don, Everett, and Bobby? They were Yankees. The Yankees team had a problem. Many of the parents noted signs of anxiety—squirming and discomfort—in their children as the players approached the field. Several Yankees could never seem to find their equipment; others developed muscle and tummy aches before every game. Although they never voiced the truth, they were afraid of the bullies, like Don, who made their Little League experiences painful, like Everett's was. Their fear was well founded, as no one was in control on their team.

The Yankees coach did not realize that his hands-off attitude and lax behavior was allowing the children on his team—his charges—to be hurt. Their pain was not from physical injuries that would leave visible scars, but from invisible wounds to their confidence and feelings of security. He was not teaching trust, order, and mutual respect; he was not providing them with an atmosphere of harmony—his greatest of all responsibilities. All was chaos on his team, and in chaos, children do not flourish—they cower.

## Harmony Can Work

The positive, safe, mutually respectful environment I call *harmony* builds a nurturing atmosphere that allows good feelings and positive self-regard to grow. These ingredients of self-confidence and discipline help children do their best. A harmonious atmosphere also teaches children morality of the highest type: respect for others and consideration of their feelings and needs. When children learn to treat others as they would like to be treated, they carry the concept of unconditional positive regard with them wherever they go. One of my daughter's teachers once told me this story:

> I've never seen anything like it. The boys were rough-housing and picking on one another, when Kaycee put her hands on her hips and yelled in an authoritative voice, "Stop it, this is not very nice. No one is to hit or pick on anyone here!"
>
> All the seven-year-old boys stopped and sat down as Kaycee sternly looked them in the eyes. She went on, "Be nice, or you're *off* the team." I did not know what team she was talking about, but whatever one it was, the boys sure didn't want to be kicked off!

Yes, sometimes children do listen; sometimes they learn, sometimes they copy your behavior. What you teach them through your actions and your words is important. Words—the right words, the positive words—can build an environment of hope and safety, respect and regard.

Can you hear the harmony?

# seventeen
## The Bible

*"Thou shalt not steal"*
*(Maury Wills made his fame by stealing 106*
*bases in one season)*

Morality? In baseball? In children? Doesn't morality belong in a church, temple, or mosque?

The dictionary defines *morality* as ". . . conduct of, or relating to, principles of right and wrong . . . conforming to a standard of right behavior." How can morality have anything to do with Little League, when baseball has so many rules to tell you what is right and what is wrong? Perhaps *morality* is the wrong word to use altogether when you are talking about sports. I asked one of my coaching colleagues and best friends, "Triphone, what's another name for *morality* in baseball?"

Tri, as we call him, stroked his stubbled black beard and pondered for several minutes. Finally, he said, "Oh, that's a good one, Vince. Have you looked it up in the Little League player's manual?"

Just at that moment, a not-too-unusual burst of emotion on the baseball field interrupted our conversation. Adrian, the Cubs manager, was screaming at the umpire, who had just called Teddy out. "What the ——! Are you blind? The kid was safe! The catcher dropped the ball!"

Teddy was rubbing his eyes and crying, "He dropped the ball when he tagged me, ump."

Beads of perspiration welled up on the young umpire's forehead as the manager of the Cubs hung over him, breathing fire.

The opposing manager of the Giants, Tom, was now in the melee, too. He quickly hid the catcher behind him.

The umpire, trying to discover the truth, naively turned to the hidden catcher. "Did you drop the ball?"

The little catcher never got a chance to open his mouth. "You're the ump!" Tom bellowed. "It's not what happened, it's what you saw!" He looked threateningly at Adrian. "Grow up, stupid! You know the rules."

At that point, the catcher came out from behind his manager and began to say, "Well, I think I really . . ." but before he could finish, Tom put a hand over his mouth. "Shut up! The ump has to call it."

The umpire blushed deep pink as a torrent of perspiration poured down his cheeks. In a low and sullen voice he repeated, "He's out."

Little heads on both sides of the benches shook and cast their eyes down at the dirt. The parents mumbled in dissatisfaction.

As the coaches went back to their dugouts, I watched them carefully. Tom did not look any of his little fellows in the eye, nor did he look at the stands. He seemed to be troubled about something—maybe ashamed. Meanwhile, Adrian let spew a few expletives to the ump, and told the catcher he had better learn to "tell the truth."

Teddy, who had been called out, was still crying loud enough to be heard in the next town. "He dropped the ball, Coach! They're all liars. I hate this game."

Back in the Cubs' dugout, Teddy's teammates were kicking their gloves. One of them yelled, "They're all cheaters!" Another whimpered, "How can this happen? How can this happen?" Somehow, it was not so much what the children said but the utter disbelief and despair in their voices that hit me most.

I went over to the Giants' side, where the parents were silent and uneasy, as if they had just been caught stealing a candy bar off a shelf, or overheard arguing with their spouse by a youngster. I knew one of the mothers. Her son had played on my team several years before. "What happened, Jean?"

She told me, in a low, guilty voice. "Well, as Davy [the catcher] placed the tag on the other boy, the ball fell out of his glove. It was obvious to us all. The umpire, however, was behind him and could not see it. Davy picked up the ball again before the umpire saw what happened. All of us knew the truth."

"Oh, that's why all the glum looks," I said. "Why didn't you say something?"

"I'm just a mother. It's not my place to yell out, 'Hey, he dropped the ball.'"

"Maybe you're right," I agreed. "But what about your son? He saw what happened. If his manager and coaches say nothing, and you don't either, what has that taught him?"

"That's life," she said curtly, ending the conversation.

## "That's Life"

I must admit life is not always fair and just. "That's life" is the only answer to an awful lot of circumstances that truly are beyond our control. Nevertheless, we do have a responsibility to our children to teach them fair play, sportsmanship, and honesty—isn't that what Little League is for? Honesty is supposed to be the best policy, and example the best teacher. Children at this age often see more than they hear, and make the kind of shrewd judgments that can crop up later in embarrassing moments. That afternoon, the children saw their coaches argue the obvious, and their parents give their consent to a lie through their silence. The lesson the children learned was obvious, too: grown-ups ignore the truth and use the rules to manipulate it. As Little League parents and coaches—as members of society in general—we cannot continue to set this kind of example for our children, or the next generation of adults will not even think about being honest, with each other or us. One thing is for sure: children learn from these experiences. They learn to ignore the truth, to manipulate the rules—and to think this behavior is good and proper. After all, they learned it from their parents, coaches, and teachers.

# eighteen
## The Bright Side

*One good man can make a difference—
and so can one bad man*

Once a year, the Little League manager who best symbolizes the spirit of the game receives a trophy. Patty, a dedicated, bright, and enthusiastic league president, thought up the idea. I remember the year Joe, the Athletics' manager, won the prize.

The Athletics had two runners on base. *Ping!* The batter hit a ground ball between the first and second basemen. The umpire, behind home plate, watched as the right fielder timidly placed his glove on the fresh, dewy grass and let the ball run into it. He then quickly picked up the ball and threw a strike to the astonished first baseman—just a second too late. "Safe!" the ump yelled.

With the umpire's attention on the first-base side, Eric—being inventive, as children will be—tried a sneak play. Running from second, he decided the best way to make home plate was a straight line from shortstop to home. As the umpire turned, he saw Eric in the baseline passing his dugout, with his teammates cheering him on toward home. The second ump, behind second base, had also missed Eric's clever base running.

Eric touched home plate before Kiel, our big first baseman, could throw the ball home, but Alex, our third baseman, started jumping up and down. "Hey mister, he missed the bag! Hey, he missed the bag!"

Joe was coaching third base. He had seen what had happened. All the youngsters had seen it, as well as the parents on both sides. Our guardian angels had seen it, and I'm sure God had made a note of it, too. It had been obvious. It was also obvious, though, that Joe and his team needed this run. The game was in its last inning and would decide who would win the second-half championship. If Eric was called out, the Athletics would have two outs and would still need two runs.

I looked at Joe. He stared intently at Alex, who now had tears in his eyes. Joe's eyes went blank, and he turned away. The ump did not know quite what to do when our shortstop, Stefan, chimed in, "He cheated, he cheated."

Joe called Eric to come over to him. He placed his hand on Eric's shoulder right in front of the dugout, where his teammates were sitting. "Did you touch third base, son?"

"No," Eric said meekly.

"Well, you'd best tell the umpires that, because they didn't see it."

Eric went up to the home-plate umpire, who towered over him like Goliath over David. In a soft, innocent voice he said, "I didn't go to third base, sir. I just ran home. I'm sorry."

The umpire patted him on the back. "Honesty is what baseball is all about. You're a real sportsman, Eric."

The ump called me and Joe over, and said, "Look, I have to call them like I see them. I didn't see him run out of the baseline or miss the bag. I must call him safe." He then announced this to all the players. Joe, however, insisted that the play be called the way it really occurred, for the benefit of the children.

As you can imagine, in addition to all the contented chatter from the parents on both sides, the Little Leaguers learned quite a lesson that day. They saw an adult stand up for the truth, even when it might cost him the game and the championship. My respect for Joe rose considerably. I don't know if I would have had the same courage to do what was right, rather than hide behind the rules of the game. With one move, Joe taught his players that honesty was more important than winning.

I have played against at least one hundred coaches in the past twelve years, but it is funny—only Joe, and a couple of bad eggs, stick out in my mind.

I recommended Joe for the Little League Manager of the Year

Award that season. Everybody else who played against him did, too. Joe exemplified what we wanted our children to learn: honesty and integrity. Too bad what happened that day occurs so infrequently.

## Rules Are Meaningless Without Truth

I do not think incidents like the one with Joe are so rare because most people are basically dishonest. Rather, I think many parents simply do not have an overall *sense of morality*, that compulsion to do what is right even when the rules say it is okay to be wrong. I do not think these parents recognize what they are teaching their children, either.

One father, for example, referring to what Joe did, said, "Well, it is not what is right or wrong, it is what the rules say."

Another agreed. "You are out only when the ump catches you. If you fool him, well, that is smart baseball."

After the game, though, Joe had said, "If I don't set an example for my little team, and insist on telling the truth and being honest, then I have taught them nothing. After all, later on in life, who will ask them if they stole a base, or shagged a fly ball, or fooled an ump? Everyone, however, can tell an honest person from a cheater."

Joe is right. It does not take long, for example, to assess someone's integrity in tennis, golf, or cards. Children do not learn integrity from lectures, they learn it by watching the most important adults in their lives—their parents. The fellow who constantly misses line calls in tennis is teaching his child to do the same; the accountant who never misses a number when he is adding up a bill, but cannot seem to add up a score above par for any hole on the golf course, is instructing his child to play "smart"—not fair. You know your assessment of these people— do they really fool anyone? Do we really think we are fooling our children? Sometimes saying nothing is worse than telling an outright lie.

# nineteen

## The Golden Rule: Sportsmanship

*You cannot prevent birds of dishonesty from
flying over your head, but you can prevent
them from building nests in your hair*
                                    *—Asian proverb*

Big tears welled up in Paul's eyes as he was called out by the
angry umpire. "Never throw the bat again," the ump barked
sternly.

The Hawks' coach yelled, "He should be thrown out of the
game, too."

Oh, yeah, I thought. I'm sure that win-at-all-costs coach would
like to have my best hitter out of the game for good.

Paul, a power hitter for T-ball, had the dangerous habit of letting the bat fly at the end of his swing. It was too bad; his hit had
gone over the left fielder's head, a sure home run.

As Paul came to the dugout, I knelt down to his eye level and
lifted his little chin. "Paul, there are rules in Little League. One of
them is to hit the ball off the tee. The second is to run to first base
after the ball is hit. The third is: never throw the bat. If you throw
the bat, you will be called out. If you don't, you can run around all
the bags and get a home run, and then everybody will be happy.
Most important, Paul, is that by throwing the bat, someone can
get hit and seriously hurt. See, that is the real reason why we
have this rule."

"But it just hit against the fence, it didn't hurt anybody," he protested.

"Paul," I said gently, "would you like a bat thrown toward you?"

"No, Coach."

"Well, if you wouldn't want it done to you, remember that the umpire and the catcher who are back there don't want it done to them, either. Someday, your bat may hit them."

Paul looked at the back fence. "Yeah," he said. "I'd be scared if I was back there, too. I wouldn't wanna be hit."

He walked away with a contented look—he had just learned a very important lesson. Not a lesson in hitting, running, or catching, but in the Golden Rule of Sportsmanship, the most important lesson of all: Treat others the way you would like to be treated.

A dark-haired young tot with bushy eyebrows, Paul was now out in the field, playing at the pitcher's mound. Lauren, from the Hawks, hit the ball to him at the mound. Paul scooped it up and stopped. Lauren ran as hard as she could to first base. "Safe," the umpire cried.

"What?" yelled Paul. "She's out! She threw the bat!"

The ump looked up and saw the bat against the fence. His puzzled face seemed to be saying, "What do I do now?"

Paul yelled assuredly, "The rules say you're out if you throw the bat." Lauren had, in fact, thrown the bat as hard as Paul had thrown his.

The ump shook his head. "No, Lauren is safe."

Disbelief crossed Paul's face, followed by tears of frustration.

I felt obligated to intervene. I told the umpire that Paul wanted to understand why Lauren was not called out when she had thrown the bat. I beckoned to the Hawks' coach, Mr. Cox, to step in, as I knew he had seen what happened. Unfortunately, I also knew he needed this run, and that he was a "play by the rules as long as it is to your advantage" kind of guy. He, of course, said, "The ump has to call it. Let's get on with the game and stop this BS."

The umpire explained to Paul that he hadn't seen the bat thrown. Paul learned the hard way the difference between the rules, and the rules as seen by the umpire. He walked to the dugout under a dark cloud. I could see the confusion on his face. It was there during the whole inning, as he pounded his glove. Seven plays later, he was still muttering to himself, "The rules say you're out. I could have been hurt by that thrown bat."

By now my knees were getting sore, but I knelt down once again to Paul's height. He still looked angry. "Paul, you just learned something very important—the difference between what is right and what are the rules. You were right; Lauren was out because she did something dangerous. But there is another rule, which says the umpire must see it."

As parents, we need to help our children understand sportsmanship. Sportsmanship is always doing what is fair, what is right, what is one's duty. Going only by the rules often makes us fall short of sportsmanship and our obligation to the truth. Mr. Cox knew his player had thrown the bat, and, in all fairness, she should have been called out, as Paul had been. But he used the rules to get around what was fair. We must try to make our children understand this important difference, so they will grow up to be like Joe of the Athletics, instead of like Mr. Cox of the Hawks. Yes, sportsmanship is a question of morality—and Little League is one of the best places for children to learn values.

We, as managers and coaches, must recognize that Little League rules are guidelines first, to ensure fairness and safety, and then establish the rules of the game, such as three strikes and you are out. If the managers and coaches mutually agree that a play was miscalled, I believe the umpire should be allowed to reverse his call based on the integrity of these adults and the need to demonstrate real sportsmanship on the baseball diamond to young, impressionable minds. That would reinforce the concept of honesty being the best policy. These children are not professional ballplayers, and Little League is not about winning baseball games. *Little League is about fun and growth and learning life's important lessons.* To teach sportsmanship, one of life's most crucial lessons, we, the coaches, managers, and parents, must all agree to emphasize its cardinal rule: how you play the game is more important than anything else—even the game itself.

# Section Four

# LIFE'S
# LESSONS

The best preparation for tomorrow is the proper use of today. Baseball is about more than hitting, catching, and the ball game itself—it is also about love, encouragement, support, and knowing when to let go. *Character, not talent, determines one's destiny.* You can foster that destiny by realizing that you cannot change the child God gave you—you can only change your attitude to him or her!

# twenty

## Prepare Yourself for the Nitty-Gritty

### *An ounce of prevention is worth a pound of pain*

Coaches can virtually recite the rules and regulations noted in the *Official Little League Guide*. They usually advise parents to read it to learn about playing Little League baseball. If you were to plod your way through it, you would know a lot about a little, and very little about the nitty-gritty of what you need to know. What you would find is:

1. Shoes with metal spikes or cleats are not permitted.
2. All Little League bats must be official Little League size: not more than 33 inches in length, not more than 2¼ inches in diameter, not less than 1⅙ inches in diameter at their smallest part.
3. Home base shall be marked by a 5-sided slab of whitened rubber. It shall be a 12-inch square with two corners filled in so that one edge is 17 inches long, two are 8½ inches long, and two are 12 inches.
4. Sleeve lengths may vary for individual players, but the sleeves for each individual shall be the same length . . . huh?
5. Any part of an undershirt exposed to view shall be . . .

Isn't this trivial? Well, yes—and no. No, because children must learn that discipline and rules help everyone have an equal opportunity. Yes, because in the development of a child, do you really think it matters how he or she is dressed, or what his or her sleeve length is?

This chapter is really about the nitty-gritty of preparation—not the rehearsed, Hollywood version, and not how you imagine Little League will be. I am talking about the down-and-dirty truth of where the game begins.

## The Great Equipment Scavenger Hunt

Preparation for the preparation begins at home. Is it important? Why, yes—possibly even more so than the game. Your preparation, Mom and Dad, will actually set the tone for the game. It is all your choice and under your control—sort of. I offer the following story in an attempt to save you from having a similar, unforgettable experience. If you have never had a child in Little League, you may find it somewhat farfetched—but if you do have Little League kids, I am sure you will find yourself with sweaty palms and a parched mouth as I take you down Memory Lane.

My son had a weekday game, and I had just rushed home from work to get him there on time. Although my body was in the front hall, my mind was still in the office. "Vinny, are you ready? It's time to get to the baseball field. Remember, I told everyone to be there twenty minutes before the game starts. Make sure you tighten your belt buckle. I'll meet you in the car."

"Okay, Dad, I'll be ready in a minute."

I patiently beeped the horn once, and my Little Leaguer skipped gleefully out of the house with his tanned-leather fielder's mitt tucked neatly under his arm. He eagerly jumped in the car, his face beaming. "Let's go, Dad."

I looked him over. "There's something missing, Vinny. Your hat —where's your hat?"

Absently, he said, "My hat. Oh, my hat."

"Yes, your baseball cap."

"Huh? I don't know, I had it before."

In a fatherly way, I reminded him that he cannot play without his baseball cap. "Run in and get it." Faster than lightning, Vinny raced through the front door of the house, which he had left open. I glanced at my watch. I could still be on time if he hurried and the lights were with me. Two minutes ground by. My work anxieties dissipated as I drummed my fingers, waiting. I beeped the horn twice—one a chirp, the second an unconscious warning blast. My grip on the wheel tightened as my back muscles followed suit.

Ah, here he came, and with his cap. As he skipped past the open door, I noticed, for the first time, his sneakers. "All Little Leaguers must have rubber cleats, or they will not be permitted to play," rumbled from deep within my cranium.

"Vinny, where are your cleats?" I said as mildly as I could, although it came out rather strained, the "eats" of *cleats* ending in a grunt. My son looked down at his feet.

"Gee, I don't know."

Brow furrowing, nostrils flaring, I now gave the issue of my loins the unequivocal message that he had done something terribly wrong. "Where did you leave them? They must be in your closet! *Get them now!*"

Off he trotted again, albeit at a somewhat disheartened pace.

The back of my neck was, by this point, as hard as a brick. My hands were riveted to the steering wheel. My neighbor glanced over from his easy chair on the porch. He saw a grown man sitting in a parked car, looking as if he were doing 236 mph in the Indy 500. I glanced at my watch once again. Even if I caught all the lights, took the shortcut behind the strip mall, and drove 236 mph, I would still be late! My neighbor fell off his chair as the horn darted out three blasts. No, no, no, I told myself, almost in the same rhythm, I will not lose control.

Vinny had gotten the signal. He once again ran past the open door into the car, one cleat tucked under each arm. Instantaneously, I realized how much easier it would be to dart out and close the door myself than remind him. Back in the car in five seconds flat, my pulse now 140 (not necessarily from the dash to the door), I zipped out of the driveway and pulled into the street. My son looked up timidly, no doubt reading my facial expressions like a video-game monitor. It was time to be quiet and meek, or else.

I heard a thump, but there was no time to stop—probably just the neighbor's cat. . . . A car, coming in the right direction at the wrong time, just missed us. I took it in stride, since my pulse was already maxed-out. This was a matter of life or death! If I was even two minutes too late, the consequences could be disastrous! All the lectures I had given the other parents, all the reminders about being on time—what would they think of me now, late, late, late, when they had busted their you-know-whats to get there at the appointed moment? I just had to be on time!

As I sped toward the field, I told Vinny to put his cleats on.

"Dad, I can't get the knot out," he whined mildly.

Oh, no! Not The Knot! How do they do it? No wonder he would just slip his shoes off and leave them. Too bad they could not just be slipped back on. Houdini himself could never have unraveled the knots Little Leaguers get in their shoelaces.

Out of the corner of my eye, I saw a street person stare as I sped down the road, steering with one hand and fighting the knot of the shoe in my mouth with the other. Have you ever tasted clay? Even the street person was gagging!

Yes! The field. We had arrived. I spit out the shoe, abruptly slowing down so I could pull into the parking lot gently. Vinny raced across the field to greet his friends, while I said hi to another parent in my most hypocritically casual voice. She cheerfully answered, "What a beautiful day for a ball game."

Just as the past ten minutes of anxiety seemed to be ebbing away, Vinny came racing back across the field to stop in front of me, his face a mixture of fear and excitement. Before he got up the courage to say anything, though, my mind's eye did a fast reverse. I recalled him jumping into the vehicle with his two cleats, one tucked under each arm. I also remembered him carrying his nice, shiny, brown-leather glove back into the house as he went to get his hat. Did he ever bring it back out? My mind flipped through the scenes in rapid succession, over and over. Yes, my worst fear had been realized. No, the rage that had me in its gnarling grip was not totally irrational. No, I definitely needed to resist the impulse to shake my wife's kid until the stuffing came out of him.

I looked at Vinny, he looked at me. He knew what I was thinking—he could feel it. Like a five-year-old, I could not hold it in—I had to say it.

"Where is your glove?"

The obvious! Yes—I asked the obvious. What's more, I knew the answer. He knew the answer. Every mom and dad in the country knew the answer, but I had to blurt that out, too. "You left it at home, didn't you? Didn't you! *Didn't you!*"

Of course he did. Why do we have such unwarranted, out-of-control responses to such obvious and incidental mistakes? Well, okay—maybe you would not have that kind of response. Maybe I am the only father who ever wanted to strangle his child the sixteenth time we went through this scavenger hunt in one season. Maybe I was the only "jerk" parent to ever inhabit Little League.

But I doubt it.

### *They* Are the Children, *We* Are the Adults, *They* Are the Children . . .

*A young child has a short attention span.* He lives in the now, the present. Past and future are adult concepts. Children do not begin to participate in activities on a regular basis without your reminders until they are about nine or ten. Even then, of course, they do not necessarily recall what they are supposed to do, nor will they necessarily do it, should they happen to remember. Baseball is a wonderful opportunity for you to teach your child good habits. On the ball field, the coach will hit ball after ball, encouraging your youngster with the same monotonous instructions every time: Keep your glove down. Get in front of the ball. Cover the ball with your hand. Take your time throwing. We parents need to use the same techniques, the same monotonous encouragements at home to reinforce the pre- and post-game instructions: Get your hat. Find your cleats. Get your glove. Put everything in the bag. Put the bag in the car.

Yes, I am a respected medical professional—but I am also a

jerk. Not until halfway through my second season did I realize the problem was not my son, but me. Children are normally disorganized. We must help them learn organization—but that did not finally dawn on me until my third year of coaching.

## Schedules and Stuff

The two most common questions asked by parents at home concerning Little League are "Where is the schedule?" and "Where is your equipment?" Here are some hints I had to learn the hard way. First, make two or three copies of the baseball schedule and put them in obvious places, such as on the kitchen door, the refrigerator door, or on the calendar, placed at your children's eye-level. If it is on the refrigerator door, it will get seen an average of eighteen times a day. If you are a mom, double that number. (By the way, sticky refrigerator doors are not uncommon as the cause of shoulder and neck pain in women.)

Displaying the schedule constantly reminds your child of the next game and keeps you from having to call the coach or team mother to find out where and when you are supposed to show up. Remember, though, most children do not know how to read a calendar. You must teach them to cross off each day so they can tell when the big game is coming.

The best way to prevent the weekly Great Equipment Scavenger Hunt is to buy a baseball bag. All sports stores have them. They are long and thin with a special zipper compartment for the bat and enough room for all the equipment. They cost between twelve and twenty dollars. You can also use an old school bag, or Dad's old army duffel.

When do you place everything in the bag? As soon as the game is over and you reach your car. Get everything from your child before he goes running off to get a snack, knock his friends' hats off, and chase the other players around the field. This is normal behavior for Little League children. They have just sat quietly in one place, the cage, for an hour and forty-five minutes without bashing one another over the head inadvertently with a bat, making mud pies near the water fountain, or rolling in the dirt. Once the game is over, they need the release of going a little wild. Their memory, though, seems to get released with their energy.

"Where is your cap?"

"Uh, I dunno."

"Where is your glove?"

"Over there, somewhere?"

"What happened to your shoes?"

"Uh . . . uh . . . uh . . ."

"Where is your head!"

We cannot expect our children to act like adults—especially since the cries of "Where are my keys?" and "Has anybody seen my appointment book?" often compete for the same airspace as "Which one is your hat?" The time to start the right habits—*your* habits, Mom and Dad—is as soon as the game is over. Grab your child's glove. If he is under eight, grab his hat as well, but let him carry his bag to the car.

Step two comes at the car. Off go his cleats, which you clean on the pavement by hitting them against the ground and, yes, untying the knots in the laces. Place all the items in the bag. Put the shoes in a plastic garbage bag if you do not want them to mess up the rest of the equipment. Next, neatly fold up his hat, then store the glove. If he has a ball and bat, make sure they get in the bag, too. Once home, make sure his belt is placed in his bag, along with a new set of socks. Now he is ready for the next pregame check.

Go through all the equipment in the bag again the day before his next game. Why? Because he will have taken the glove and hat out during the week to play. In time, you can remind him to check his own equipment. If you see him do it by age nine, you can bask in the glow of having a precocious child. If you succeed by the time he is six, my guess would be: 1) he was potty-trained before he was two; 2) by the time he is thirty-five, he will suffer from constipation and hemorrhoids (just as you do); 3) you are one of those type-three parents I described in a previous chapter; and 4) you found that this chapter, and many others in this book, does not relate to you. If so, read "Parental Expectations" again at the end of the season. If it still does not make sense, then either you are not human, or you are in deep denial and need *a lot* of therapy.

Little League is great when you are prepared, Mom and Dad— and when you realize that you are not alone.

## One Last Hint

Many children, caught up in the frivolous fray of post-game euphoria, inadvertently wander off and get lost. Do not expect them to remember their own telephone number. Write it on their shoes, glove, and hat. By the way, hats are often misplaced and unintentionally taken, especially early in the season, when they are all clean and look the same. Later on, you will be able to recognize your child's belongings by the mustard, catsup, and other indelible stains they manage to acquire during the season. Nevertheless, do not leave responsibility for your child's possessions up to your child, unless you have a saintly amount of patience and an infinite limit on your Visa card.

# twenty-one

## Participation, or "Does Da Cheering Matter?"

*There's those that make things happen*
*Others who watch what's happening*
*And others who wonder what happened*
*—Tommy Lasorda*

Mr. Hall yawned, and Mrs. Gallagher nodded off as yet another Little Leaguer missed the ball sitting on the tee. The benches were fairly empty. Mr. Sanchez stretched out to get some rays. Mr. Habid tapped his watch and put it to his ear to see if it was still working. If a pin dropped, you could have heard it among the parents sitting dutifully in the bleachers. Their bodies were there, but their minds were asleep.

Have you ever been to a Little League game where the arguments of the managers and umpires were louder than the cheering of the parents for their children? Just what does parental participation in Little League mean—and does it really matter to the outcome of the game?

Baseball is unique—it has no cheerleaders. Go to a basketball game and you will find a pep squad arousing the fans at crucial moments to urge their teams on to triumph. Of course, no sport demonstrates the use of cheerleaders for generating crowd participation more than the behemoth sport of football: *"Hold that line! Hold that line! Defense! Defense! Go Team!"* Pom-poms twirling, the head cheerleader leaps ten feet in the air, coming down in a perfect landing with arms outstretched for victory to the thunderous ovation of a thousand or more fans.

Ask Jimmy the Greek—or any casino—if home advantage is a prominent factor, and he will tell you the odds are always with the hometown prizefighter, player, or team. Check your own newspaper tonight for the home-vs.-away statistics in any sport, and you will find a definite difference, be the game baseball, football, basketball, or hockey. Generally, the scores favor the home team by about 70 percent. In college basketball, for example, many teams go undefeated at home year after year. Is this due to the ball or the basket, because the length of the field is different, the weather is better, or the lighting is different? Probably not. Is it the exuberant cheering and applause of the home crowd— those thousands of fans yelling and screaming? Unquestionably, yes!

What does cheering do? Medically speaking, excitement and encouragement heighten the release of adrenaline, which is stored in little bubblelike vesicles. When released into the brain and bloodstream, adrenaline increases alertness, muscle tone, readiness, pupillary size, breathing capacity, and cardiac output. All these physical body reactions are needed for the human body to react optimally to its environment. In other words, when excitement and encouragement release adrenaline and other hormones into our systems, we get stimulated to a state of peak psychological and physiological readiness, prepared for any eventuality. In simpler terms, you can tell if children are at their best by the skip in their step and the gleam in their eye. To doctors, that skip is the adrenaline in their arteries going to their muscles, and that gleam is the epinephrine in their wide eyes. *Cutting edge, momentum, intensity, focus,* and *concentration* are not just words; they are actual body reactions.

Since we know these physiological characteristics of readiness, why are too many Little League games so slow and lackluster that the only response they engender at times is a good yawn? Well, when was the last time you saw a cheerleader at a Little League game?

## Back to the Padres

Top of the first inning. The Padres' parents were huddled together in the stands, full of anticipation, their eyes riveted on their own youngsters. Vinny was up first for the Padres. He smacked a dribbler to third base. The ball was caught but overthrown. The Padres' parents cheered. Next, Patrick hit a long ball to the outfield. The parents were on their feet waving, clapping, hooting with joy. The face of each Padre's parent beamed with pride. The little ballplayers with bright yellow Padres hats stood proud, their chests trying to protrude out of their oversized uniforms. If you asked them who they were, they would have screamed in unison, "Padres!" As each peewee player crossed the plate, he was met with the enthusiasm of all the team moms and dads. The children skipped around the bases; they all had a zing to their swing. The adrenaline was flowing, the epinephrine coursing through every muscle.

One and a half hours later, bottom of the sixth. The Padres were now on the field, the score 21 to 19 in their favor. The Hawks, though, had already scored five runs this inning, with two men on base and three batters to go. The Hawks' parents were in a frenzy. Sparks of their enthusiasm were igniting their little batters. Gary, the next Hawk to bat, strode up to the box with determination, and pounded the plate with his bat. Adrenaline coursed through his arteries, coming from the Hawks' parents and coaches chanting praises and encouragement: "Hit the big one! Clean the bases!"

In the stands, on the opposite side, a gray cloud hung over the bleachers. The faces of the once-proud Padres' parents had turned sour. They sat cowering, as if sleet and rain were pelting down on their heads, as if they just had heard Lou Gehrig tell them he was leaving baseball. The Padres themselves were slump-shouldered and droopy-armed as if drenched, already accepting defeat. Their gloves looked more like anchors than instruments for catching a speeding ball. The spigots of their adrenaline had been turned off, both in the stands and on the field; their tanks were on "empty."

Jimmy peered out from under his cap at his mother and father sitting there glumly, wringing their hands. Some moms and dads were slowly shaking their heads no. Jimmy's heart threw a big tear up to his eye. I guess I am bad, he thought, a real loser. Look how sad I'm making Mom.

Neither he nor the team parents were conscious of it, but those adults were conveying a definite message to Jimmy and all his teammates. The juice, the momentum was gone—the smell of defeat saturated the team. Had the parents' behavior affected the children, or the children's playing affected the parents?

## Three Cheers for Cheering

Labeling these parents as "losers" is an easy out. Sure, what these children needed is obvious, at least in hindsight, but how many times have you cheered your team on when it was losing? Logically—which is how all adults think—one would not cheer if the Dodgers or the Yankees or the home team was getting trounced and had lost its juice. Logically, then, one also would not cheer—meaning, be happy—when one's own kids were getting beaten. The problem is that children do not understand logic the way we grown-ups do. Losing is just not as important to them as it is to us. They are more interested in the fun of playing the game, and having something to be happy about. When we tell them differently by our disapproving mood, who really loses— our kids or us? Who has their priorities right, who is being logical? We know that cheering and encouragement turn up adrenaline, which gives children the focus and spirit to do their best. Logically, then, when we do not cheer, we are the ones being illogical.

Cheering is not simply a way of rejoicing when the team is doing well; it is a way of showing acceptance and love and giving children a vote of confidence—*especially* when things are not going as hoped. *Children need praise the most when they appear to deserve it the least.* A child's self-concept (what he thinks of himself) depends on the reflection his mom, dad, and other significant adults, such as coaches and managers, give him. This is why some children are so confident with themselves despite their shortcomings, while others are so discouraged about their abilities despite all their gifts. Cheering when the child or team is doing well is also definitely important, of course, as it encourages repetition of the behavior and enhances self-confidence. Cheering when your team is down is even more important, because it specifically augments the physiological response that increases physical prowess, to make your child the best he can be. In other words, cheering *is* the home advantage.

## Cheering Is Winning

After my second year as manager, I could plainly see that children with positive, participating parents had winning teams. Pick the right parents, and you had a team that loved to play, a team in which, at the end of the season, everyone was looking forward to getting back in the game the next year. To me, a winning team was parents who would bring love, affection, and a touch of tenderness to their kids. The children were secure, and cooperative with their friends. Nothing was boring to them. They seemed to have it all, because their parents were always at their sides to guide and mold them into beautiful, harmonious sculptures with genuine grins and hearts full of contentment.

These children did not cringe with grief because they missed a grounder or overthrew first base. They knew that if they made the effort they would always be rewarded. Their parents' cheers were not rewards for the runs scored or the plays made; they were hymns of support, trumpets of solidarity behind their children. The glee that emanated from these kids as the Little League season rolled on was the music that made me come back to coach year after year.

# twenty-two
## Choosing a Coach

***He who has no fire cannot warm others***

Mary turned as the door opened and her husband, Reginald, meandered in without looking up or greeting her. "What's wrong, honey?"

"You know that car I've been looking into?"

"Which one, Reginald? Our bedroom is covered with flyers from the hundred-or-so dealerships you have visited in the last two months. Our dresser is overflowing with every automotive magazine published in the past two years!"

"Well, I had decided to buy the Lanca 2AQXRM-7 Turbo, so when I saw one in the parking lot this evening at the Pavilion, I waited until the owner came out. When I asked him how he liked it, he said it was the best-looking car he had ever owned—it was just too bad it spent more time in the dealer's garage than in his! Mary, I am so tired of looking for a car. The harder I look, the more confused I get."

"Well, think about something else," Mary advised. "Little Reggie made a Little League team. You have to drop him off at the field tomorrow. His coach's name is Trisant, of the Dodgers."

"What'd you say?" Reginald responded absently. "Mr. Tyrant from the Dodge dealer? I don't remember looking at any Dodges, though I hear Chrysler cars are really good this year."

Somewhat exasperated, Mary said, "No, Mr. Trisant of the Dodgers."

"Listen, Mary, Dodge doesn't make a Triumph, that's an English car." Reginald saw his wife grind her teeth together and realized he had better stop. He had really misheard her at first, but the second remark was supposed to be a joke—one Mary obviously did not appreciate. Changing to a serious tone, he said, "I'll drop Little Reggie off at the field, and maybe while I'm waiting, I will visit the Dodge dealer—it couldn't hurt."

Reginald drove Little Reggie to the field the following morning and spotted someone wearing the Dodgers team hat. As he got closer, he noted a slightly built middle-aged man, whom he figured must be the coach. "Hi, my name's Reginald Fender. Are you Mr. Tyrant?"

"Trisant," said the coach. "Is this your kid?" He turned to Little Reggie. "Run out to the field so I can hit some balls to you."

Little Reggie, all seven years of him, skipped out to the field.

Reginald turned to Mr. Trisant. "You'll keep him entertained for an hour or so?"

"Yeah."

"Well, I'll be back then."

As Little Reggie reached the field and turned, he saw his dad walking toward the parking lot. The gleam in his eyes dimmed, the smile on his face drooped. He had imagined all night that he and his dad would be together. He so wanted his dad to be with him. "He didn't even say good-bye." Little Reggie sighed. "I guess I'm really not so important to him. What did I do to disappoint him?"

Most parents give little more time to inspecting their coach than Reginald did—they spend more time choosing tomatoes at the market. Like Reginald, many think Little League and its coaches are nothing more than baby-sitters. The coach you walk away from and leave your child with, though, may have a tremendous influence on your child's future, not to mention his or her like—or dislike—of sports. Remember your child's sign: NOTICE ME. TELL ME I'M IMPORTANT.

### It Only Takes One "Rotten Apple" Coach

Shea was assigned to my team in my fourth year of T-ball. I did not know him prior to that first day, but I can still see him in my mind's eye, dragging his little body out onto the ball field—he was the image of a prisoner of war. I could have sworn he had a ball-and-chain on both legs as he shuffled out at a snail's pace to shortstop. Shea's dad, I saw, had creases of concern all over his face. I yelled encouragingly to the infield, "Are we ready?"

All but Shea yelled, "Yes!"

As I hit a ball to Shea, he bent over quite adroitly, scooped it up, and threw a strike to the first baseman. Wow! "Great catch, great throw," I yelled. Shea's head lifted a little, and I thought I saw a flash of a smile.

When our practice came to an end, I went over to Shea's dad. "Your son is quite talented. How come he looked like he was going to the dentist when you brought him out?"

"Shea had a terrible experience with baseball his first year," his dad said. "I literally had to carry him to this first practice. He didn't want to play at all; I practically had to force him."

It seemed that at the previous year's first practice, Shea's coach had made an example out of him in front of the other children for talking out of turn. The coach ordered Shea to do ten push-ups. When the boy just stood there, the coach yelled at him until he cried. The coach thought Shea was being disrespectful, but Shea did not know what a push-up was. His first-year coach had no idea that a six-year-old could not possibly do ten push-ups, even if he did know what they were.

Remember, a coach is often a coach simply because he was the only one who accepted the position. Many coaches, in other words, get the job by default. Coaches and managers do not have to pass an interview—they only have to say yes to the league vice presidents and presidents, who are frantically trying to coax someone into the position for the following year.

Parental and coaching expectations can differ greatly, and, as we know, the coach is not the only one who may have distorted objectives and expectations. The least a mom and dad can do is call ahead to assess the attitude of their child's potential role models. In the same vein, the coach must be ready to confront the parents' expectations if they are potentially unhealthy for any of the children.

Though you might not realize it, your being there has a special significance to a child between the ages of five and thirteen. Children's dreams are mainly focused on their mom and dad's love, approval, and time spent playing with them. If you are not there, your approval and love are not apparent to them. Children must see and feel your presence, not imagine or "accept" it on your word. If you doubt your importance, just look into the eyes of your child. If you do not see any love, look into a mirror at your own eyes—they will show you what your children are seeing.

## Time for New Mandates

How can Little League help assure that parents make adequate coach choices? First, by requiring a pre-team meeting. Second, by letting parents know the essential questions to ask. Third, by requiring first-time coaches and managers to undergo specific training to learn:

1) Basic norms of child psychology and motor development at the different ages of Little Leaguers. A child hit in the face with a baseball thrown by a teenage coach, for example, will most likely be discouraged from trying again.
2) Basic training in pitching, catching, and hitting.
3) The ingredients and importance of sportsmanship. This is what will make them excel, with or without athletic talent, and (hopefully) make our country a better place to live!

Remember, approximately 40 percent to 50 percent of all six-year-old children cannot catch a ball thrown to them on a fly. Up to 50 percent of them who had never played baseball before, in fact, would be in dire danger of getting hit by it. A coach who does not realize this can traumatize those kids in the very first practice, making the rest of the season an uphill battle. Having well-informed coaches is important. Having coaches with appropriate priorities is essential. Organized Little League must place this as its top priority.

# twenty-three
## Stuck with a Coach

### *Never tolerate the intolerable*

The Athletics were having a wild time. Billy had just filled Wesley's hat with water and dumped it on his head, drawing laughs of derision and taunting from his teammates. Wesley did not seem to enjoy being the brunt of this prank. He slowly wandered off, the tears welling up in his eyes, hidden by the downpour of water still dripping off his brown locks.

Mrs. Haynes viewed the mayhem from afar, unaware of her son's dilemma. She glanced impatiently at her watch. The coach wanted everyone there twenty minutes before game time, but it was now five minutes before the official start and he had not yet arrived.

Mrs. Haynes finally caught a glimpse of Mr. Cox, the coach, lumbering toward the field. He toted a large, bulky, green-gray tattered canvas bag that hung over his shoulder and made him look like Santa Claus with a baseball cap. Huh, more like the Grinch Who Stole Christmas, she thought.

As he approached the chaos on the field, he barked, "Why aren't you guys warming up?"

Jimmy let go of Shannon's hair, and she dropped his hat. Mark swallowed the water he was just going to squirt all over Wesley. All the grinning faces quickly turned to stone.

He's late for the tenth time this season, Mrs. Haynes said to herself, and he's yelling at the kids? Why, he is not only totally unreliable, he takes out his own mistakes on the children. They were just acting the way kids do when unsupervised.

Mrs. Haynes weighed the idea of saying something nasty to the coach, but decided against it. Wesley, her son, was quiet and not overly coordinated, but very loving and obedient. He had been practicing hard with his dad all week for the chance to play second base. The coach had been promising him for the past ten games that he would get to play second "sometime," but the season was ending, and so far, Wesley had still not gotten his chance.

As Mr. Cox scribbled down the lineup, Mrs. Haynes timidly approached him in the dugout. "Mr. Cox," she pleaded, "Wesley has been practicing very hard all week so he could play second base. Do you think you could put him in for maybe an inning? I don't want to jeopardize your winning, but it would mean . . ."

Mr. Cox cut her off without looking up. "Look, your son can't chew gum and walk at the same time without tripping or falling. I'll put him where I want him!"

Mrs. Haynes was crushed and outraged. What an insensitive oaf, she thought. He does not care about me, much less my child —and here I have entrusted my only son to this man. If only Wesley's dad were here!

Before she could regain her composure, Mr. Cox turned to bark at the kids again. "All of you get over here and listen up. Remember last game?" All the little stone faces nodded. Actually, though, most of them did not remember it. Children are blessed with the present. Their recall for the past can be easily erased, unless something very traumatic happens, or we adults hammer their mistakes into their memories. Grown-ups are often stifled by the past and blinded to the present because of our anticipation of the future. We mistakenly expect that children think as we do. Wrong! Experience is in the eye of the beholder—especially for the young. An unforgivable error in the professional leagues is a good try and a positive effort in Little League. Remember five-error Tony?

As the children looked blankly at Mr. Cox, Mark smiled a little. "What are you smiling about?" the coach demanded. "You see what that dog did over there on the ground?"

Mark looked at the small brown heap, and his smile quickly dwindled to a frown. I am sure he missed the innuendo, but Mr. Cox's crabby face certainly drove home the message. Off to the side of the dugout, Mrs. Haynes's mouth dropped open in disbelief. Mr. Cox was more insensitive and degrading than any Little League coach or manager she had ever seen. She looked at the eyes of the children. They must all feel awful, she thought. Is this supposed to be building confidence in these children, in my son?

Believe it or not, Little League coaches and managers inflict these kinds of abusive remarks and unrelenting expectations on their players repeatedly, every year. As a coach, you must realize how much damage you can do in the few months you have charge of your little team members—even in only a few hours a week. As a parent, you must learn to recognize unwanted and destructive behavior and do whatever is necessary to protect your children from it—even if it means rocking the boat. After all, Mom and Dad, you are ultimately responsible for who teaches and cares for your children. How much fear and self-condemnation do you want them to learn?

## The Good, the Bad . . .

Mr. Cox yelled, "Get out on the field for practice." He snatched a bat out of the bag as if it were a meat cleaver, pointed it at Mark on third base, and hit a zinger that Mike Piazza would have had trouble fielding. The ball hit Mark in the chest, knocking him over. "Use your glove, not your mouth, to stop the ball!" shouted the coach. "Get up and try again, and don't let me see any crybaby crap!"

Mrs. Haynes, now thoroughly horrified, looked about for a man to take charge and sock the SOB—or at least cripple him for a day or two—but she and Mrs. Reyes, who spoke hardly any English, were the only Athletics' parents attending the game.

Parents of the opposing team, however, filled the bleachers on the other side and were doing a chorus of cheers. "Two, four, six, eight, who are the kids we appreciate!" They named each child on the team in turn, ending with, "Yes we think you're great!" and "Go, Pirates, go!"

Mrs. Haynes came over to the Pirates' dugout. The coach was kneeling down to be at eye height with his Little Leaguers. He wore a big smile and spoke softly, yet emphatically. "You looked great out there in warm-ups. I've never seen such a talented team in all my career," he said earnestly. The kids had heard this many times before, but loved it as much now as the first time. He then reminded them that they were playing a good team and should always respect their opponents. He told them to try their best, never give up, and remember that he was always proud of them. He ended with, "Who are we?"

They shouted in unison, "Pirates!"

"Who?"

"The Pirates!"

"Let your mom and dad hear you!"

With all the gusto in their tiny lungs they bellowed, "The Pirates!"

The coach jumped up and whooped, "Let's get out there and have some fun!"

The players sprang out of the dugout and ran cheering to their positions.

Mrs. Haynes walked over to look at the Pirates' lineup board. She had seen it at each game hanging at the Little Leaguers' eye level, right at the entrance to their dugout. A magnetic board etched with a baseball field, it had little magnets with each player's name stationed at his or her fielding position. To the right of the field were similar magnets with each child's name and nickname. Up first was Charging Charlie; second, King Kim; third Rock 'Em Rachel, and so on. Each nickname engendered positive regard, marking some particular asset the child possessed.

Mrs. Haynes's sadness deepened. Why did my son get stuck with such an irresponsible, insensitive, negative-attitude, unprincipled, dumb coach, she thought, when other teams had such good, positive, caring team leaders? Coach Cox rarely had practice, and when he did, he showed up late. He never taught the children how to field; he only criticized them for missing the ball. If they did catch it, heaven help them if they did not make a good throw. When someone made a good play, his compliment was "About time you did something right," or "Like I taught you." When the Athletics were on the field, his only words of encouragement were "What are you doing? Wake up! Are you sick or do you just look that way? Get the lead out of your pants." Wesley had twice asked his mom not to put lead in the washer, as he was certain his coach saw it in his pants.

The coach had favorites, too—not that he treated them much better. Mrs. Haynes knew that the league president had constantly monitored Mr. Cox last season when he had coached in the minors, because he had a tendency not to place children in the lineup who deserved to be there. He knew it was a Little League rule that each child must be up at least once and play a minimum of two innings every game. Mr. Cox would have players change uniforms so the opposing coach would think he was actually playing all his children.

## . . . and the Ugly

Top of the first inning. Our third batter was up with a man on first and second, and one out. Rock 'Em Rachel strode up to the tee. The Pirate bench chanted, "Let's go, Rachel, let's go!" and stomped their feet, *boom, boom.*

Cox stepped out and bellowed so loudly, the major Little League, three hundred yards away, could hear it. "The fat girl is up. She's slow as molasses. Let's get a double play."

His little Athletics giggled. Mark, on third base, chanted, "Let's go Fat Girl, let's go!"

One tiny tear welled up in Rock 'Em Rachel's eye. Her cherub grin turned into a wounded-puppy pout as the other Athletics all giggled and chimed in. "Let's go Fat Girl, let's go Piggy!" For the first time, Mr. Cox smiled his approval.

The Pirate coach called time out, walked up to Rock 'Em Rachel, kissed her gently on the cap, then strode slowly toward the Athletics' bench. The bleachers, filled with nurturing Pirates' parents, gasped. The two thirteen-year-old umps could only cross their fingers. They did not know what to do. No rules had been broken.

The coach continued his methodical, determined journey across the field.

"Let him have it, just once—for me," Mrs. Haynes muttered softly.

Mr. Cox's snarling bulldog stance changed to the tremulous cower of a frightened poodle. Standing close to six feet, and weighing 210 pounds—not much of it fat—the Pirates' coach had a somewhat intimidating stature. A hush fell over the field; the air was so taut, no one dared cough. Thunder was expected, with lightning to follow—Rock 'Em Rachel was the coach's daughter. As Mrs. Haynes bit her nails in expectation, the Pirates' coach raised his mighty right arm and placed it over Mr. Cox's shoulder in a fatherly gesture. He whispered in Cox's ear for about thirty seconds, patted him on the back, and walked away with a grin. When he got halfway back to his own dugout, he chanted, "Let's go, Rock 'Em Rachel!"

The children, at first frightened, relaxed their shoulders, and the game continued as if nothing had transpired. Mark blurted out again, "Let's go!" and was swiftly reprimanded by Mr. Cox. "Shut up and play the game."

Rock 'Em Rachel hit the ball flush; it darted through the infield to the outfield fence. Rock 'Em trotted around to third base, where she danced around Mark, who was now quiet and solemn. Rachel, however, only smiled, and waved at the cheering bleachers filled with adulating parents. One of the parents yelled, "What was that?" and the Pirates' bench jumped up: "Nice hit!" As the next Pirate trotted to first on a well-hit ball, the coach yelled out, "Who's the father or mother of that kid?" Both parents stood up and received an enthusiastic ovation from the other parents.

"What I saw," Mrs. Haynes later told me, "was the children cheering for one another, the parents all being there for their kids. Every time something occurred, good or bad, they found a way to say something positive. I'll never forgive myself for not asking more questions before letting Wesley be coached by that awful man."

Mrs. Haynes did not know it, but the Pirates' coach knew she had been at all her son's games; Wesley was on his list to be drafted the following year. He was not interested in talent—he knew that would come along if the child was encouraged. What Mrs. Haynes did know was that no matter what the score, the Pirates always won. Each child and parent came away with unconditional positive regard for themselves and everyone else on their team.

# twenty-four

## One Rotten Apple Spoils the Bunch

*One "voweluable" coach is worth a thousand consonants*

The year after Wesley Haynes played for the Athletics, we lost almost 20 percent of the children from the preceding Little League season. The children had not moved out of town, been eaten by space invaders, or gone on drugs. They and their parents had just had a bad experience—usually with the coaching staff. At the heart of the problem was Mr. Cox, the win-at-all-costs coach. Umpires hated officiating his games, since he would invariably run out onto the field to disagree with a call, and other coaches—afraid of another confrontation, another argument—had nightmares the day before they were going to face his team. Cox's players had, predictably, taken on his attitude and demeanor. They would call the umpire "four eyes," or "blind as a bat." Some of the other managers decided that if they could not beat him, they would join him; soon every game involved at least one confrontation. Little League was not a game anymore, it was a hard, bitter lesson in the dog-eat-dog realities of life on the battlefield. At times, the diamond looked more like the floor of the New York Stock Exchange or *Divorce Court* than a home-town baseball field.

This was not just my imagination. The telltale signs spoke out clearly. Parent participation dwindled. Coaches arrived late—not just the ones facing Mr. Cox, but Cox's staff, too. I am certain he did not enjoy these confrontations any more than those who had to face him did.

## How to Find a Good Coach

Mrs. Haynes had gone to all her son's games just to try to undo Mr. Cox's role-modeling, but she had not taken her son off the team because it was her first year, and she did not know any better. Some parents take their children out of Little League permanently before they realize they can have a choice in picking the man or woman who will become an influential part of their child's life. You do have the choice. Look for a coach who has the right *A-E-I-O-U* (and *F):*

**Attitude.** Coaches should have an attitude of positive regard and loving encouragement for all the children, parents, and umpires. This attitude is conveyed in expressions like "good play" and "nice try," especially when a child has made the proverbial error.

**Enthusiasm.** A good coach has the ability to bring out the best in children and their parents. This spirit is often catching. The children capture it and take it with them wherever they go. You see it when they cheer on their teammates who are up to bat, when they encourage their pitcher. Enthusiasm keeps children focused and is the chief ingredient in having fun. It is the "2-4-6-8, who do we appreciate," the "High five!" the welcoming smile and ready handshake.

**Integrity.** Integrity in coaching means having principles that encourage cooperation and mutual respect. It means sportsmanship—always winning, even when you lose. A coach with integrity is the type of person your child can look up to, the coach who makes you feel good about yourself and whom you want to be around. He's the coach you hope your child will grow up to be like.

**Objective.** A good coach is someone who clearly indicates why he wanted the job and what he expects the parents and chil-

dren to get out of his coaching. He will let you know his objective is to create a positive experience for your child, one that
will enhance motor skills, psychological and moral development, and future growth. Such an objective puts winning games
second in importance to teamwork and spirit, and reminds you
why your children are in baseball. Listen to this coach and you
will hear, "What is best for the children?"

**Understanding.** A good coach listens and understands the needs
and expectations of each child and parent. A good coach understands his need to be reliable. A good coach gives your child
adequate practice—at least once a week for T-ball, and twice a
week for farm, minors, and majors. This coach is considerate
and understands the need to follow through with his promises.
He treats all members of his team equally; he makes you feel
comfortable. His words are "How is your child doing? How are
you doing?" He gives as much praise to those that play the
bench as to the "stars" on the field.

**Fundamentals.** A coach should know baseball in general and the
rules of Little League in particular. Even more, though, he must
know how to teach the basics of pitching, hitting, and catching
to little children, who may be afraid of the ball or smaller than
the bat they are trying to swing.

## Go for the Vowels

Which of these attributes is most important? In T-ball, farm,
and minors, the coach's prior baseball know-how is a lower priority. What good is a well-trained Little Leaguer if he is not a good
sport and a team player? Ty Cobb, for example, the greatest hitter
of all times, was despised by many of his contemporaries. Yes, he
was phenomenal—a real "winner"—but his undying love of "winning at all costs" was his only unique asset. Most who wrote
about him had little to say about his honesty and integrity. A drive
to win, of course, is highly regarded and encouraged in American
sports: "Winning, there is nothing like it." And I agree—*if* you are
a professional, and *if* your job and livelihood depend on winning.
Hopefully, those who reach the pro level have been nurtured
along sufficiently to become meaningful citizens who offer a

wholesome example for our children after their professional sports careers end. As recent headlines attest, though, some sportspeople who are successful due to sheer talent have been trained to win regardless of what it takes. Once their career is over, unfortunately, they often continue that self-absorbed trend and wind up as gamblers or alcoholics, unable to get along or nurture others to become all that they could be. Trained to be skilled athletes who win, win, win, their own emotional growth was actually stunted. They never fully developed, either psychologically or morally. These stunted athletes are the has-beens, the flashes in the pan whom the world quickly forgets. Their mistake —and the mistake of their parents—was in developing only their talent, not their character. I'll never forget something my dad said often as I grew up: "Talent will get you to first base, but character is what you need to get you home."

Even when you know what to look for in a coach, you still have to find that person. Start by calling your league president. Little League officials hear all the complaints of parents, and usually know who they would like their own children to be coached by. Give a lot of consideration to their recommendations.

Second, ask other parents who have been in the same league. You can find a list of them in the *Official Little League Guide*, published annually. Never feel you are imposing when you call a stranger about your child. Just think of the rewarding experience you may be giving him or her. Remember Reginald? He did not think twice about waiting to talk with some stranger about a car. Certainly, selecting an adult role model for your child is at least as important.

Unfortunately, the coach often picks the child rather than the other way around. You can, however, influence this decision. I have seen requests by parents who specifically asked not to have their child be coached by certain managers and have gotten their wish. This may hurt the manager's feelings, but it may also alert him that something he does needs correcting. If the choice is between getting the best for your child or protecting an adult's feelings, there really is no choice, is there?

### Should Women Be Coaches?

"Moms as managers will be the demise of Little League Baseball!"

"How can they ever hope to be good male identity figures!"

The truth is, moms cannot be male identity figures at all—but they can be good managers.

Some of the best managers and coaches I have seen in T-ball and farm have been women. Some of them had scant actual baseball know-how at the start, but they had tons of *A-E-I-O-U:* positive attitude, enthusiasm, integrity, objective, and understanding. What they did not know about teaching the children how to hit and throw, they managed to learn within a remarkably short time.

Women often have reliability, wonderful objectives, and principles. They are seldom burdened with old baggage from previous bad competitive-sports experiences, because they probably didn't play Little League as children. They have no macho image to uphold and are not threatened by the manly man's "king of the roost" hang-ups. They are simply tuned in to the children. I remember a perfect example of this. I was sipping hot coffee at the snack bar on a Saturday morning, when I was suddenly shaken out of my daydreams by the usual fracas that seemed to accompany any game that involved Mr. Cox and his current team, the Hawks. On this particular occasion, his face was going through a rainbow of angry colors as he threw down his hat and raced across the field to third base. "You blind *bleep-bleep!*" Cox screamed. "He was safe by a mile!"

Mrs. Rose, the Indians' manager, calmly walked over to the scene. Mr. Cox turned on her with fists clenched, but before he could utter another obscenity, she said, "I agree with you, Mr. Cox, but do we call it as the umpire saw it—as you have insisted on in the past—or do we do what is fair?"

For once, the Hawks' manager was stunned into silence. Mrs. Rose continued in a soothing tone. "Really, Mr. Cox, if you were my child, you would get a spanking for throwing tantrums like this. I do not even tolerate such behavior in my five-year-old. What will the children think?"

Mrs. Rose's calm, matter-of-fact honesty totally disarmed Mr.

Cox—the only time I had ever seen him speechless. With no ax to grind or unresolved conflicts or pride to interfere with protecting the children's best interests, she reduced what would normally have been a classic nose-to-nose confrontation into a gentle lesson in manners.

If someone were to ask me the best combination for a Little League coaching staff, I would pick a mother with a little baseball experience for manager, and two males for coaches: one a father, the other a grandfather. I would want the mother for her sensitivity, attitude, and objectives; the father for his fundamentals and knowledge of baseball; and the grandfather for his wisdom. Grandfathers can distinguish the dash from the marathon, and are ready to slow down and have fun with their grandchildren.

Why do Little League presidents and vice presidents have to frantically search for coaches each season? The most common reason is the time element. People simply do not feel they have enough extra hours to make the commitment. As a doctor, I, too, had to give a lot of consideration to this problem. I have found over the years, though, that anyone can find the time to coach, if he or she is complemented by dependable, supportive parents and other coaches. Believe me, I may have lost some patients (that is, some potential patients), but my children and I will never regret the time we spent together. Although it has become a cliché, it is nevertheless true—in all my years as a physician, I have never heard one elderly patient regret that he or she did not spend more time at the office. I have heard them lament about the time they wish they had spent with their children. I, for one, will never regret the time I spent on the baseball field at Hamilton Park—nor will my children.

Sometimes the person souring the beauty of Little League is not a parent or coach—sometimes it is something much bigger, ominous, and destructive: the Ice Men.

# twenty-five
## The Ice Men

*Break the ice, don't become part of it*

No, I am not going to discuss the Neanderthal men who lived in the Ice Age, or the behemoths occasionally found frozen in glaciers. However, the Ice Men of Little League can make you feel just as cold as an ice cube, and the power they wield is often more frightening than any charging behemoth could be. The most frightening part about Ice Men is that any of us can be transformed into one—and, even worse, we often accept the designation gladly and feel honored at joining their ranks.

Vinny, six, and Kaycee, three, hopped out of the van at our very first midseason father/son-daughter Little League party, held at the annual Fathers' Softball Game.

"Wait here," I warned, watching out for other cars. "Hold my hands." I tucked my glove under my arm, looked both ways, and hurried toward the field with Vinny and Kaycee dangling from either arm.

Vinny's eyes were as wide as an owl's as they took in all the pageantry of the booths to the left and right, the knock-down-the-bottle, the ring-toss, and the other games. The scent of cooking burgers mingled with the sweet odor of chili sauce drew my attention as I looked down at my late thirties abdominal bulge that hung precariously over my belt, as if it might fall off and plunge to the ground any second.

Over to the left, some of the moms were setting tables; to the right, a number of children dashed after one another playing tag.

In the center stood several major-league coaches whom I recognized, although as a T-Ball coach I had never had an opportunity to actually meet them. Vinny and Kaycee quickly ran off to play. My wife, Arlene, was still trying to get little Mike, just four months old, ready, and would follow in a couple of minutes.

Oh, what a day for a ball game, I thought, and I took a deep breath and let the mixture of sweet aromas cross my palate again. Somewhere inside me, though, fluttered a small twinge—stomach butterflies, which I recognized from my years in competitive sports. Imagine, a Little League softball game, and I had butterflies! In my defense, I knew Vinny and Kaycee would be seeing their dad play ball against people his own age for the first time. I didn't want to disappoint them. I smiled, which gave me some small insight into how they must feel when I watch them. I spotted Tri, my T-Ball comanager. "Hey, Tri, ready for the big game?"

I could barely believe it, but I could see a little tension in Tri's eyes. "Sure, Vince," he said, somewhat tightly.

I moseyed over to the major-league coaches, and stuck out my hand. "Hi, my name is Vince." One of them, about half a foot taller than me and dressed in jeans and a Giant's shirt and cap, gave me half a glance and continued with his conversation. I stepped back a little from the blast of cold air, and looked at the six of them standing there. The one who ignored me had his hands on his hips as if ready to give orders from the bow of a ship. Four others nodded reassuringly, and laughed haughtily. The last one folded his arms, gave me a half smile—more of a smug smirk—and looked about as if all that lay before him was his domain. His glance went right through me; my skin felt like it was rippling as goose bumps jumped through to the surface. Even the warm California sunshine could not overcome the chill I felt.

I decided my frosty reception might just have been a lukewarm entry. Not wanting to seem uninterested and too brash, I thought I should just listen. Chuck, the six foot two arm-folder, cast his icy glance over the playing field. "Frank, your son may just take us to the state playoffs this year." The Giant-shirt-and-cap shook his head as Chuck continued. "If we don't win it this year, from the looks of our new prospects, we'll never do it."

"Ah," I said, spotting the perfect opening. "I'm Vince Fortanasce, new manager of the T-Ball Padres, and coach of the new prospects."

Since I was staring him in the face, Chuck had no way to ignore me now. For a second he returned my stare, straight into my eyes. I could see the wheels turning as he glanced at my head, then at the substantial paunch I was developing. The brief flame of combat in his eyes then went ice cold. "Hi. I hope you can develop some talent out of that little bunch." He then dismissed me with a quick turn to the others, "Let's make up a lineup," and the six of them drifted away in a group. One man, shorter than the others, trailed behind to smile and shake my hand.

"Hi," he said. "My name is Billy."

The stands were full as we dads took to the field. The Ice Men, as I learned to call them, divided up—five on one team, Billy on the other. Although Chuck called out the sides and I was picked last, I landed on his team. To my surprise, I got put in as third-base coach. "Oh well," I muttered to myself, "better than the bench."

The game proceeded somewhat differently than I had anticipated. Instead of a friendly game of softball, it was a hotly contested match, with each dad playing as if his life depended on it. There was no horsing around, no friendly chatter—only tobacco chewing, foot stamping, and grunting. Some of the older youngsters openly commented on "how pathetic" some of us dads were. Gee, these kids aren't kidding, I thought. Where did they learn to be so critical?

Third inning, the score was 8–4, I was still coaching third base. All of a sudden, Nathan, one of the over-the-hill Ice Men, slid all six foot five of himself into second. He immediately rolled over, clutching his hamstring. I ran over, thinking that now was my chance. Announcing my physicianhood, I took charge, briefly examined him, and helped him off the field. The next inning, Chuck begrudgingly pointed at me to take Nathan's third-base position.

As I stationed myself out there, I glanced at Vinny, Kaycee, and Arlene, who was holding Michael. Somehow their smiling faces made sense, and warmed some of the terrible chill running up and down my spine.

Tri strolled to the plate. I yelled, "Hey, Tri, hit an easy one to me so I can look good."

Tri smiled and called back, "I don't know if I can get this old body to turn that far around to get it to you, Vince."

I glanced toward Chuck at shortstop as giggles came from the stands, the first sign of a healthy humor since the game's inception. He did not seem amused. "Keep your mind on the game!"

I instinctively gulped as a thread of fear crept through. Then I realized, "This is stupid." At that moment, with a man on first, the ball was drilled my way. Reflexively, I stabbed at it, pulled it in, and fired it toward second. A little high, but a perfect toss to the right fielder.

The stands moaned. My grin faded as a small black rain-cloud gathered around my head. A little piercing voice announced, "Nice stop, dad. That's getting in front of it." There with Kaycee right next to him was Vinny, his little fingers grabbing through the fence, their four eyes swelling with pride.

They're proud of me! I suddenly realized. They don't care if the throw was wide! Chuck and the other Ice Men, however, definitely did not have the same look. Their eyes were steely cold.

Moments later, to my conscious but not demonstrable glee, we were losing 8–10, and guess what—I was up, with two men on.

In the dugout the Ice Men fretted. Apparently, the rest of their team was nothing but a burden they had to carry. One Ice Man openly remarked, "The bottom of the lineup. I guess we'll have to wait until the last inning to score some runs."

Another one admonished me, "Two outs, two on . . . just get on base any way you can."

I thought, gee, if that's the case, maybe I should have brought my gun.

As I stood at home plate, I could feel Vinny's, Kaycee's, and Arlene's eyes riveted on me. "Hit one for pop, pop," Vinny yelled. Oh, the pressure! An emergency room full of head injuries sprawled all over the gurneys would be nothing compared to the pressure of that moment. I came back to reality just as the ball whipped right by me and the umpire yelled, "Strike!"

"That's it, pick the one you want, dad!" Vinny squealed. Funny how it seemed I could hear only his voice—but not for long.

"Don't strike out, for God's sake!"

"At least go down swinging!" This last was accompanied by a blast of ice from Chuck as he led off the bag at third base. My mind went blank as the next ball was delivered.

"Holy ——!" Chuck slapped me on the back and shook my hand after I had trotted triumphantly across home plate. "I think we lost the ball! You're hot stuff!" I could hardly wait to hug Vinny, Kaycee, Arlene, and Michael. The score was not 11–10, the game was not over, and I do not even remember the final outcome. As I entered the dugout, the five Ice Men now looked me in the eye with invitation and a glad hand. "What college did you play for?"

"Seton Hall," I said, shaking hands all around.

"So which one is your kid?"

I ignored the question, choosing, instead, to leave the cold behind and make a beeline to my undying, faithful fans: my family.

As I drove home that evening, I realized I was in some way one of the boys—"Hot Stuff." Two home runs had put me there. I could not help thinking, though, about those who were not "one of the boys"—those still out in the cold. Was this what Little League was all about? Certain parents forming a circle that not only excludes other parents, but other children they think are not up to snuff? "In-crowd" parents who, in their frankly judgmental way, declare, "Yeah, you've got it—that kid doesn't"? Open prejudice based on the way people look?

Through the years, I have seen even ethnic and professional Ice Men—those who, not necessarily consciously but through their actions, declare themselves to be somehow a tier above. Is this the origin of bias? Is this what we want to teach our children? Unfortunately, this middle-age pomposity does trickle down to the kids. They set up their own "in-crowd," dealing with *their* teammates in a similar fashion. Even more unfortunately, any one can be pulled into this igloo arena of the self-acclaiming Ice Men.

All of us in Little League—and life—must be aware of this natural propensity to form cliques, and the potential dangers in giving in to these urges. We must neither allow nor tolerate it. An essential part of leadership is setting a good example. Coaches, managers, vice presidents, and presidents must set examples of openness, goodwill and friendship to all—and tolerate nothing less.

Are you an Ice Man? Chances are, you are not if your team is in last place. Chances are, you are—or have the potential to be—if you are one of the All Star coaches or managers in the majors. To my dismay, this often becomes the domain of the Ice Men. If you are talented, or have a talented child, you are in a special, privileged position. You can exude warmth and friendship, or make your staff into an exclusive polar bear club. If you are unsure where you stand, ask yourself who you shook hands with at the last game, and how much time you spent teaching the second-string players. If you cannot remember, guess what—you are part of the Ice Age, and you do not belong in modern-day Little League. All is not lost, however—you can always grow up. Start now!

# twenty-six

## The Coach's Dilemma—Only Nine Can Play

*It's one thing to be in left field; it's another thing entirely to be left out*

I remember playing hide-and-seek when I was no more than five or six years old. All my friends hid, as I did. As time went by, I thought, What a great hiding spot. As more time dragged on, though, I worried, Gee, maybe I found too good a spot. Finally, I sneaked out into the open and crept toward home base, almost hoping I would get caught. I froze when I saw no one was there. All my friends had suddenly evaporated! Did the Martians eat them? Did everyone on the planet suddenly disappear? Did my mom and dad still exist? For a moment, I was terrified. Then, suddenly, way down the block, I saw some movement. It was my friends. No wonder nobody found me—they had not even remembered I was there! I wept all the way back home.

As I toddled up the stairs and reached for the door knob, I started to panic. Maybe even my mom and dad had left! Tears still splashing down my cheeks, I timidly opened the door. There was my mom. She took one look at me and ran over to see where I was hurt. I did not have a scratch on me—just a broken little heart. I had been left out.

. . .

I have seen that same face on my Little Leaguers in the farm system, minors, and majors. Fortunately, the T-ball league solved the problem by ensuring that everyone play each inning. T-ball has thirteen players, thirteen fielders, and thirteen batters up each inning. After T-ball, though, there are still twelve to thirteen players on a team, but only nine may participate in the game at any one time. Of these nine, only one can be pitcher, one cleanup batter, and one catcher.

One of the toughest situations in life is to be left out. When a coach makes out his lineup, however, that is exactly what he does—he leaves three to four players out of the game for at least a small amount of time. This is a disheartening and sometimes unbearable situation, both for the children and their parents. My knowledge, and my own experience of having been left out as a child, made this a particularly tough situation I had to face at every game. Although there is no easy way to overcome this hurdle, you can do some things to help soften the blow.

## Three Cheers for the Cheerleader

Make bench participation important by rewarding the child who does the loudest, happiest cheering for his team from the dugout. During practices and games, point out the ones who cheer on their team as much as those who play the field. This way, the benchwarmers feel equally as important as the fielders. Giving a special-recognition spirit award at the end of each game worked well for me. One year I gave gift certificates to McDonald's; another year, it was Big Chew bubblegum. Each child has his own special gift—often, the coach must find and develop it.

## Practice, Parents, Practice

My biggest tribulation as a coach and manager was the sad reality that not every child can play every inning, nor every child choose his favorite position. The fact that certain children are favored and get to play every game—and often the entire game in farm, minors, and majors—is a reality of life. Stress the need for those playing the bench to put more effort into practicing with their parents, and give them special instructions on how they might improve their game. Children need to have a sense that they can better themselves with effort and be rewarded for it. These children typically have not played as long as the others, are not as naturally talented, or, more commonly, have not yet physically matured to the point of their teammates. Encouraging their parents to practice with them is of utmost importance—it shows that Mom and Dad have not given up on them and accept them as they are. Specific drills also give the parents something concrete to work with and hope for. During team practice, make sure these children get their full practice time with the coaching staff, too—otherwise, they will really feel left out, not even good enough to practice with the team.

## Greg Played the Bench

Greg will always remain in my mind as a child who had so little, yet did so much with it. I selected him for my team after the Little League commissioner told me he was going to advise Greg's parents that Little League might be "too dangerous" for him. I had to agree, the child was awkward. At almost eleven years of age, he still could not throw the ball well enough to reach first base. His mechanics at batting were somewhere between golf and handball. What he had, however, was the biggest smile, greatest attitude, and most conscientious parents on the team.

Greg never became an all-star, but he did become a leader. Greg led the cheers. He often went over to encourage the more talented players after they had struck out or dropped an easy fly ball. For this, he was liked by all; the more talented boys would often take time out to teach and play with him. He never could swing a bat, but he eventually learned to bunt. He stayed out practicing with his dad every night, and by mid-season he was catching fly balls. Not once did he ask or demand to play as much as the other team members. His response, when I asked if he would like to play the whole game, was a big smile. "Yeah, but I got to practice more first."

Greg's was an unusual story, but not implausible. His parents were positive, hard-working, and realistic. They knew who they were, they knew their son's talents and weaknesses, and they did not delude him into believing he was something that he was not. They encouraged the gifts he had: sincerity, caring, and a warm heart. They supported him in his efforts to be what he was— loved and lovable—and their satisfaction with him radiated through his smile. "You cannot change the color of your child's eyes," his father told me, "but you can change the way they glow."

## Willard Could Never Do Enough

On the other end of the spectrum was Little League's greatest loser: Willard. An intense little boy, Willard was an average player with an average build. Whenever a line formed, though, he would push his way to the front. Whatever position he was in, he would want to play another—usually first base, or one of the other difficult positions on the field.

When Willard did not get his way, he would run to persuade another coach. If he was taken out of the game, he would run to his parents and complain rather than cheer for his teammates. His parents, very attentive, were always asking why their son was taken out, since, they claimed, he could play whatever position he was put in and was obviously better than his teammates—especially those in positions they deemed destined by fate for their son.

At first, I spent a great deal of time trying to help Willard's parents understand the rationale of team spirit and participation. Then I exposed them to the reality of life—not all children are given the same talents. Finally, and most important, I talked about the concept of timely self-fulfillment: a child's confidence must be accomplished in steps. The first step is for the parents to accept their child for who he is and what talents he has, not for the talents they believe he should have. The second is to encourage him to improve himself—which, once again, depends on their approval. In time, their acceptance and his hard work will lead to the child's self-fulfillment—to his being all he can be, satisfied with himself.

Self-fulfillment cannot be pushed. Placing a first-grader in the fourth grade, for example, would obviously destroy his self-confidence as a student and athlete, as he would recognize his inability to compete with the older, more mature, and larger children. Recent studies, in fact, have shown that children who are moved up a year in school often lack the necessary physical prowess and sociability to function well at the higher level, and frequently have poorer self-concept and confidence than if left to mature at a normal, timely pace. While they might do well intellectually, there is more to life and child-development than grades.

In Little League, to follow the same line of reasoning, it is better to be a big batter in a little field—better to play the minors and grow than be pushed into the majors and doomed to failure.

I explained to Willard's parents, therefore, that placing him on first base, where he might miss many balls, could hurt him, and reinforce a negative image, causing loss of confidence. I wanted first to put him in a spot where he could feel good about himself and gain confidence, then move him up to more difficult positions as his skills improved. They seemed to understand.

I arrived a little late for the next game. There at first base, to my dismay, stood Willard, where his parents had persuaded my assistant coach to put him. They had told him, in fact, that I had promised to place him there this game.

After four straight errors, my heart bled for this little trooper, who so wanted to make his parents proud. He, though, like they, was heavily armored. As he came in, he berated the other boys for throwing the balls too low, too high, or too soft.

When Willard got up to bat, the usual chant, "Let's go, Willard, let's go!" was absent. When I started the cheer, the other players quickly reminded me to stop. "He doesn't like anyone to cheer. He says it causes him to strike out all the time."

I stopped and watched as Willard let the third strike go by. As he turned, I saw more than dissatisfaction in his eyes—I saw an empty void. He could not face anyone, especially his parents. He was only ten years old.

All Little Leaguers want to pitch. In an effort to be fair, we would give all the players the chance to pitch at practice, and count their strikes and near-strikes. In succeeding practices, I found myself spending an inordinate amount of time trying to help Willard learn to pitch, but I was never able to satisfy him. He eventually did improve overall, however, and I finally felt he was ready for first base. Fortune smiled on that game—only a very few plays were made to first base. In the two plays that did come his way, Willard did very well. I looked at his parents; they seemed pleased.

"Well," I said to myself, "persistence pays off. Now maybe I can pay attention to some of the other players on the team." Before I could say Rip Van Winkle, though, Willard announced I should put him in as pitcher the next inning.

At that point, a little voice in the back of my head said, "Enough is enough. There are twelve other players." I patted Willard on the back and told him what a great job he had done, but I was putting Steve in to pitch. Willard actually seemed relieved with my answer. Steve did his best. Despite walking three and giving up three hits, he came out with a big smile, his dad and mom cheering. I was satisfied, he was happy—this was what Little League was all about.

As I congratulated the other team players and walked off the field with a contented smile on my face, I mused that I had finally given my little players the opportunity to have their dreams come true. Suddenly, my sugarplum thoughts were squashed—the league president motioned me over. "I have to talk with you in private. It seems some of the parents are upset with you for letting other boys pitch and 'deliberately' keeping their child out. I watched, and I must say, the pitchers you used did not seem any better than this child. Are you playing favorites?"

The smile on my face faded. "Really," I said from between clenched teeth as a thunderstorm erupted behind my eyes and lightning bolts shot out from both ears. "Could those 'some parents' be Willard's?"

Patty, a gifted woman herself, smiled at me in amusement. "Why, yes. And they are inciting other parents to ill-content."

I could only feel sorry for Willard. Nothing he could do would ever be good enough for his parents. Worse, he was being taught to project his shortcomings onto others. Even worse than that, he was learning he could intimidate people and possibly get his own way through manipulation. Yes, he had gotten a greater share of attention than most of the other players, and, yes, despite not proving himself more than the others, he had manipulated his way into positions that caused him pain and loss of pride. Now, on a day that he had finally succeeded and done well, his parents dashed his glory by letting him know it was not a first baseman they wanted, but a pitcher. Critical parents spawn malcontented children.

## How to Deal with the Impossible

What should a coach do under these circumstances? Bench the kid? Banish him to right field? Trade him to Cox's team? That would only punish him for his parents' lack of maturity and sensitivity. Instead, I decided, a good coach would teach the child to recognize when he was content with himself. "Willard, did you enjoy playing first base? You did a really good job out there. I was proud of you." My hope was that by reinforcing his good job at first base and reminding him how important that position was, he would start to feel good about what he could already do. I sometimes ask children, "Which is the most important wheel on a car?" No matter what they pick, I shake my head. "All the wheels are important. If any one of them does not do its job, you will not get where you are going. The same is true with a baseball team. Each position is important." You, the coach, must make your team players and parents understand this. A coach's influence may be momentary compared with a parent's, but it can be the beginning of change for the child.

Now, how should a coach handle the parents—tell them when the next train leaves? Ah, if only you could sometimes! Coping with parents is much more difficult. Discontented children are usually spawned by their supercritical parents. All a coach can do is ask, "Are you satisfied with your child?" If they say yes, then confront them with how they continually show dissatisfaction about their child's place on the team, and how his behavior affects others. (They may need to examine their own relationship with their own mothers and fathers. This type of parent often needs professional help, but will rarely seek it.) You must learn to recognize these parents and act in unison with the other coaches against such destructive behavior, or the parents will divide you against one another. Any Little League coach can attest to how one Know-It-All family can ruin the whole season.

## Only You Can Make Life "Fair"

Parents teach team spirit and help build maturity when they advise both their star-player and benchwarming children to root and cheer for the other teammates on the field. Sowing dissension and dissatisfaction in a child indicates a lack of maturity on the parents' part, and merely reveals their inability to deal with shortfalls or shortcomings. Children who learn to make the best of their situation—like little Greg, the cheerleader—grow up self-contented. They learn that attitude is what makes something fair or not fair—not the thing itself. Having to deal with such hardships as sitting on the bench while the others get to play teaches children how to cope with adversity and helps build character.

Parents, make the most of the situation your child finds himself in. Give him encouragement and, more, your time. If your child has practiced hard and done his best to succeed, tell your Little League coach of his efforts. Most will try to make those efforts bear fruit. A lot can be accomplished if you proceed in a timely manner that builds confidence in your child, step by step. The days of Little League are when you can most influence your child toward the path of independence. By age thirteen, many children no longer cherish their parents' attention; you will probably find your influence crashing like the 1929 stock market. Do not be like so many parents who recognize, too late, that they have already let the most important time of their life with their child slip by. Their only memories are regrets. A happy memory is a joy forever. Make your dreams come true—start making happy memories right now.

# twenty-seven
## Dreams

*Baseball in the heart puts sunshine in the day*

The phone startled me out of a deep sleep. Rubbing my eyes, I stretched over to pick it up. "Hello?"

"Hi, Uncle Vin? It's me, Mark. I didn't want to wake you too early. It's eight-fifteen in the morning there, isn't it? We just had a son at five-fifteen! What a feeling it is! I can't begin to describe it. When I held him in my arms and gazed into his eyes, for the first time I realized what life is all about!"

I checked the clock next to my bed. It was 2:35 A.M., California time. My nephew used to be a good ballplayer as a child, but he never did have any sense of time.

"I've already gotten him a glove, bat, and ball," he went on. "I just can't wait to get him out of the nursery and onto the ball field."

That line brought me wide awake. The ecstasy in Mark's voice, the joy, the hope—I knew Mark was imagining the very same thing I had when my first son, Vinny, had been born. As soon as I realized it was a boy, I had started dreaming of tossing the ball to him and having him toss it back—the beginning of bonding, that invisible magnetic force that forms an inseparable link between parent and child, which often occurs later for fathers than for mothers. In America, the true relationship between father and son often starts with baseball. The ball field becomes their first common ground. Baseball is a time for sharing and building memories, for fathers—and now mothers—to impart their knowledge to their child. Baseball is more than a ball being tossed to and fro

—it is love and acceptance being passed back and forth. Poems are written about the game, books and films are centered on it. "If you build it, he will come," the movie *Field of Dreams* claimed, and every young ballplayer in the country understood. The gleeful squeals of a child, the warmth and pride that kindles in the heart. . . . Oh, this is the dream of every dad who ever played Little League baseball. I have seen it in the children—a spark in their smiles, an ember that glows and grows as we parents nurture it into a steady flame of strength and resiliency. Every father knows the feeling. My dad once told me, "You never know the meaning of life, of love—of anything—until you have a child and play ball with him!"

Yes, I knew what my nephew was feeling and dreaming. I also knew, as you do, that once Thomas James, my new great-nephew, came home from the nursery, Mark's life would change in ways he probably had not imagined. Sleepless nights, wet diapers, endless feedings—and the quivering chin, accompanied by the tiny whimper that ends as soon as you pick him up, only to be reignited the very instant he is put down. For the time being, though, Mark was on cloud nine. His feet would collide with the earth soon enough. As I congratulated him and hung up, I put my arms behind my head and slowly closed my eyes. Oh, yes! How I had looked forward, as Mark does today, to being out there with my son. . . .

## Not the Best, Not the Worst—Just the Reality

It seems like only yesterday that little Vinny held my thumb as I led him onto the Little League diamond, my diamond of dreams. His baseball cap was skewed sideways and his glove dragged by his side, but he had a skip to his step and a sparkle in his eye. I cannot even describe the jumble of feelings I had. I positioned him like a little treasure at third base and walked over to first. I was sure I could see a little ember of contentment emanating from his smile.

Little League tryouts would be in two weeks. I would train my son just the way my dad had trained me. I could not believe it. Vinny stood there with a grin and pounded his tiny fist into the glove as he had seen me do so many times. I threw the first ball, and watched it bounce toward him. Riveting his eyes on the white sphere as it tumbled forward, he snagged it just at the precise moment, pulled it out of his glove, and threw a perfect strike.

Oh, God, if this is not heaven, what is? I thought. In the recesses of my brain, I heard the major-league loudspeaker at Dodgers Stadium: "And in the stands today is Dr. Fortanasce, out to see his all-star son playing third base and cleanup batter. . . ." I heard the chatter and cheers of the fans. I looked back at my son; I could have sworn that was a flame I now saw radiating from his chest.

My next toss was a little harder. Vinny scooped it up again, but this time threw it ten feet wide.

I retrieved the ball and approached my son with a frown of concern. I explained how to throw the ball straight, and what the consequences were of a bad throw in Little League. A bad throw was an error, I told him, which was bad. It would let a man on base, and a potential run score. Going back to first base, I increased the speed of my next throw, giving Vinny a one-bouncer. The ball careened first off the heel of his glove, then off his chest. Without a whimper, he picked it up and threw it—again, ten feet off target. Vinny smiled and pounded his glove, waiting for my next toss. I shook my head no, and walked over to third again to instruct him on the art of catching a one-bouncer, and the importance of preventing a ball from getting by you. "If you do, it's an error," I remember saying. As I walked back across the field again, I remember thinking that I'd have to increase the number of practices if he ever wanted to be ready.

Another toss. Vinny picked it off as I had told him to, but instead of throwing the ball, he just held it. "Vinny, throw the ball," I yelled. He merely looked at me and shook his head no.

"Vinny, throw the ball," I yelled a little louder. Then I noticed his face. The sparkle was gone. The flame had dwindled and died.

"Dad," he said, "let's go. I don't want to make errors."

Fatherly (and a little annoyed), I stomped over to third base. "Vinny, you will never be a good ballplayer if you don't practice."

"Daddy, I want to go home."

"Listen, son," I quickly retorted. "Life is not always a game. We are going to play for at least another ten minutes, until you get it right. Tryouts are only two weeks away."

Walking back to first, I suddenly realized I could no longer hear the announcer broadcasting my name. My grin had turned grim. Well, I thought, it is time for Vinny to learn discipline. Just what has his mother been doing all these years with him? Ten minutes of play, and already he wants to quit. Kids these days have it too good, too easy.

I reached back and flung the next ball to Vinny. He simply stood there and let the ball, all of one foot to his left, go right by him.

"Vinny," I blared loudly enough to be heard across the ball field, "what's wrong with you?"

In answer, my son started to giggle and dance about like a marionette being pulled by strings.

"Stop acting stupid," I said angrily. This remark, however, only induced more puppet activity. As I briskly passed Vinny to fetch the ball, I saw my dreams melting down into pools of disappointment.

As soon as I arrived home the next day, I found Vinny, patted him on the back, and suggested we go out to play. He said he could not find his glove. I told him where it was and would wait for him at the door. When I did not hear him coming, I went to look for him. I found him standing in front of the TV, watching the same show I had just told him to turn off. Disappointment—no, hurt—overwhelmed me. My son did not care for me. He did not want to play with his own father. He did not really care about getting ready for tryouts. He had no discipline! How could this have happened?

Need I really explain?

When Vinny was ten, he turned to me out of the blue one day and said, "Dad, remember when you told me about not making errors?"

"Yeah."

"Well, I thought if I did, someone would get hurt real bad. I was afraid if I played, you would get hurt."

He then gave me a crooked little smile and shot out the door to go play, while I stood there with my mouth hanging open. About eight years later, when I was helping him select a college, he gave me that same crooked smile and said, "You know, Dad, preparing for college is a lot like preparing for Little League. I wanted you to accept me for what I was then, and be proud of me—but I was so afraid of disappointing you. It seems I've got the same problem now."

My eyes filled with tears as I realized that Vinny's puppet routine had really been a strong, albeit nonverbal message: "Dad, please like me. Please smile. Look, look, I'm a puppet, here to entertain you." He had been trying his best, but his best was not good enough for me. My dream of playing ball with my son back in his Little League days was not marred due to a lack of discipline, but because my tone and expressions clearly told him I was withdrawing my acceptance and love. He had no idea what "preparing for tryouts" meant—all he had wanted was to have a good time with his dad. He did not want to hurt me by making an "error."

Each one of my children has had a different nonverbal way of giving me the same message. My daughter, Kaycee, would become stubborn and deliberately make the same mistake over and over whenever she felt she was not getting a favorable response from me. Michael, though, was the most difficult of all. One moment he would act as if he was too exhausted to even stumble down the baseline; ten minutes later, he would be magically restored to life. Fortunately, I took his pulse during one of those episodes, found it was 180, and took him in for some tests. We discovered that Michael had W.P.W. (Wolff Parkinson White Syndrome), a cardiac arrhythmia that can be fatal—and has been so to several basketball and football stars. Luckily, a new catheter surgery cured the problem. Of course, it also cured what I thought was a nonverbal communication. After the surgery, though, Michael developed another pattern of behavior that told me, loud and clear, "Hey, Dad, lighten up!" He began to twitch his neck and grimace, occasionally letting out a little *cheep*, like a bird. Being a neurologist, I immediately recognized this as Tourette's syndrome, a neurological disorder characterized by sudden, uncontrollable mannerisms, such as twitching, or tics associated with unusual vocalizations. I was not going to make the same mistake twice, so I quickly brought Michael in to see my partner, Charlie, a pediatric neurologist. Luckily, it was not Tourette's syndrome at all, just a nervous habit that went away when I changed my behavior!

I eventually found out that I was not alone. My interactions with Vinny, Kaycee, and Michael turned out to be mild compared with some of the things I saw. Tellingly, it was not the disinterested fathers, but the dedicated ones, who tried hardest with their children and had often been baseball aficionados all their lives, who seemed to have the hardest time. Those with the biggest dreams had the biggest problems. Even more tellingly, moms rarely had the same difficulties, I noted.

## A Bitter Fact to Face

Two days after my first dream turned sour with Vinny, I witnessed another dad practicing with his son. "Damn it! Get in front of the ball! Where's your head?"

Finally, the boy just stood still with the ball and refused to throw it—just like Vinny. His father let loose with some *bleep*, *bleep*, *bleeps*, and turned his back on his son. Seeing his chance, the boy threw the ball and hit his dad right between the buttocks. To give you a hint of what happened next, the little guy ended up on his tiptoes, holding the same part of his anatomy his father had just received the ball with. How could something so potentially wonderful become such a nightmare? I wondered. How does a father with such good intentions turn into a near child abuser?

Tri, one of my closest friends, and I coached our first team together. His son Patrick was such an obedient child—until Tri tried to teach him to play, that is. Suddenly, dutiful little Patrick would turn into a stone-faced zombie, stand totally still, and stare straight ahead with no expression or response as Tri attempted to talk to him—and wound up talking to himself. "Why won't he listen? Why won't he try?" Why, why, why, indeed! After two practices, Vinny was placed as third baseman and Patrick as shortstop. At the start of practice, Vinny and Patrick looked and acted just like our sons, but as the session progressed, a distressing metamorphosis occurred. Vinny turned from an attentive ballplayer into a giggling puppet, while Patrick, a skillful shortstop, degenerated into a mummified zombie. When we asked them what was wrong, they said, "Nothing." Did they want to play? "Oh, sure," they said with the enthusiasm of a child waiting for an enema.

Arlene, my wife, and Lu, Tri's wife, soon became concerned about how their sons dragged themselves to the ball field. I remember the day it all came to a head, just as I remember the day President Kennedy was assassinated. Vinny and I had just gotten home from practice. I was in the bedroom changing my shoes when Arlene walked in. "Vinny told me he doesn't like baseball. He doesn't want to play. I think you are the reason he doesn't like it. If you can't change how you treat him, I'm going to pull him out."

"Pull him out? Pull him out! *Pull him out!*" The words reverberated in my head. This was far beyond a personal crisis—it was more like the end of the world! I could not imagine living without a boy in Little League. Yes, I know it sounds stupid. Imagine me, a doctor, who deals with life-and-death situations every day, not knowing that life is more than baseball. But deep down, I cherished my dream. Arlene's ultimatum made me feel as if I were facing Armageddon, but it also forced me to make a decision. Necessity is the mother of invention, after all.

Deep down, I knew my wife was right, because I could see so clearly what Tri was doing wrong. Good Lord, you would have thought he was talking to a professional ballplayer out there. He never applauded Patrick's successes, only reinforced his mistakes. Yet, with my son and the other boys, Tri was a model of patience, positive attitude, and support. I, too, had nothing but praise and patience for the rest of my team, but was doing exactly the same thing with my own son as Tri was with Patrick. Looking back now, I realize I had been living a myth—well, actually, several myths.

## Fairy Tales Don't Always Come True . . .

The first myth is that *every child will naturally love baseball*. This reality only exists in the mind of the parent. Children will like baseball if they get their mom and dad's approval, or, later, as they grow, if they are very talented in it, and get approval from their friends. Initially, however, parental and coach endorsement is the pivotal issue. Every child will love baseball if his parents love and approve of him while he is playing it. My frowns, dissatisfaction, and lectures did not give Vinny the idea that I approved of or liked him. Children see their own self-worth through how we see them. Remember "we smile, they smile"? Well, when we frown, they think they are bad.

The second myth is that *our children will love playing ball with us*, which is the flip side of the coin to myth number one. Our kids will enjoy something and want to do it again if they feel they are pleasing us. The same principle continues throughout our lives. Love between a wife and a husband dwindles once one or the other feels disapproved of or not respected. Your child will continue to love playing baseball with you as long as you continue to show your love and respect for him.

The third myth is that *children always tell the truth*. For the most part, they do—but not if they feel they will be punished for it or get into trouble. I can still remember my three children—their faces smeared with icing and their fingers covered with crumbs—innocently telling me, "No, we didn't touch the birthday cake." Children naturally tell us what they think we want to hear, in order to avoid trouble. Parents and coaches must learn to look at the nonverbal messages that tell the real story. Suddenly being unable to find his glove, for instance, and getting distracted by the TV were real messages from Vinny—I was just not "listening" to what he was showing me. Each child has his or her own, unique type of nonverbal communication, or expression of anxiety or anger. One child I knew would stick her tongue in her cheek when she was angry. I frequently asked her if she was chewing gum or eating, but she would always say no. Years later, when she was in high school, I learned she did this tongue-in-cheek routine whenever she got angry. It had started when she first stuck her tongue out at her dad and promptly received a spanking in reply. To protect herself, she had developed this disguise technique, which satisfied her need to express herself and, at the same time, allowed her to avoid punishment. Some of the more frequent mannerisms children bring to our neurology clinic are tics, head twitching, forcefully closing their eyes, or clucking their tongues. Often, these are just their nonverbal ways of communicating their tension.

The final myth is that *a parent is the best teacher for his or her child.* This may be true, but only if that parent does not have unrealistic expectations or conflicts in his or her own life. Unreasonable expectations begin with unrealistic dreams. Children do not start out sharing their parents' dreams and will never grow to share them unless treated with respect, love, and honor, whether they make mistakes or not. Children have minds of their own; most often their only expectation of baseball is to have fun. They will react positively if they get their parents' and coaches' approval. One good rule of thumb is to try to deal with what you perceive as faults in your child as gently as you deal with your own; another is to do something to make your child smile when you are upset with him, and *then* go back to the task.

## Give a Little, Get a Lot

If your dreams of playing ball with your child are rapidly turning into a Stephen King nightmare, step back and take a little reality check. First, recognize the difference between what you think is the problem and what the problem really is. I thought my problem with Vinny was his attitude, but it was actually my "anticipatory anxiety." I knew the tryouts were coming up, Vinny did not—even if he had, he would have had no concept of what they meant to me. I had gone through twenty-seven years of school always preparing for the next test. My anxious mind said, "What if Vinny isn't ready for the big test? Why, he will be a failure the rest of his life. He will never learn discipline. He will never amount to anything."

Yes, these were my problems. Vinny's problem was seeing my frown and tone of voice, which told him I did not approve of him.

Vinny did not want to disappoint me—he wanted to stop playing so he would not hurt me anymore, and maybe do something else so we could be friends again.

Next, recognize your child's expectations to have fun, and make you laugh. Children really do want to make us happy, so go ahead—have fun, roll in the grass, play games. Before you can hope to teach your child anything, he must learn to like you. If you are having fun, you will be fun to be with; if you are always serious and disapproving, you will be the last person he wants to be around. When you have fun together, your child will soon want to be like you, because you love and accept him and want to be with him. Once you have his love, he will do anything you say, if it is within his capabilities. Remember, just because a child is genetically yours does not mean he will love or want to be with you. You must earn that love—and that, Mom and Dad, takes time together having fun.

Child-rearing is like flying a kite. You must run gently at first, until the kite begins to soar on its own. Then you slowly pay out the string, so it can go higher and higher. Once up, changing winds may make it necessary to reel the kite in closer for a while, or let it out even more. The same goes for children. Never worry about the severity of the wind, because a child, like a kite, flies highest when he goes against the current.

If you treat your child correctly, you will know it by the warmth of his smile, the glow of his face, and the eagerness in his stride. Next week, when Mark's feet have touched the ground again, I think I will tell him about kite flying!

# Section Five

---

# SEIZE
# THE DAY

Faith is the greatest virtue you can cultivate in your children, and the greatest gift you can give them. Never lose faith—in yourself or your children. Little League is only the first leg in their marathon of life—but it is one of the few you can totally run with them. Once that part of the journey is over, it is gone forever. Don't lose the opportunity—seize the day!

# twenty-eight

# Bull Derringer

### *We have seen the enemy, and it is us*

Bull Derringer was the nightmare of my youth, reincarnated to make me miserable as an adult. You know him. He is the ultimate know-it-all, the guy too good for the likes of you. He is clean-cut, and still in good shape despite the years. A clipboard always under his arm, he is flanked by two "yes, sir" coaches.

When I first met him, he reminded me of Billy McMann, my real childhood nightmare. You knew him, too. He was not the flagrant, beat-'em-up bully, but the kind that left scars without ever laying a finger on his victim. He was the "better than you" bully. Somehow, he was always on the winning team, always in the limelight, always one step ahead of you. He never shook hands after he beat you—he might soil his hands or his uniform. He was the only guy you knew who could slide into a base without getting dirty. He never smiled, he scoffed—with a condescending demeanor and a greater-than-thou attitude.

The only time he changed his cocky attitude was when the league president was around. Then Mr. McMean became Mr. Goody-Two-Shoes. You probably remember this hypocrite, too. To hear him tell it, he was the only guy on the team. He would have beaten you 100 to nothing if the other eight guys had not been around to pull him down. What made matters worse, he was probably right!

Somehow, every time I was around Billy the Kid, I felt bad. Something demonic stirred in me. I would have done anything just to see him trip over first base or strike out with the bases loaded. On the rare occasion when he did mess up, my guilt over being so envious would take some of the joy out of his mistake, but I knew I was not alone in my snickering. All the other players' faces would light up with glee, too. Billy the Kid could not have missed noticing, but it only seemed to make him even more determined to show me and everybody else how truly, impeccably inferior we were. No matter how often I told myself, "I'm not going to let him get to me," he always had the perfect put-down to destroy my resolve.

I remember the time I hit a home run off him. I was trotting around the bases, approaching third, when I heard his voice from the mound. "Good thing you had your eyes closed, four-eyes. Otherwise you would have missed it." Being a bright kid, I had a million comebacks—unfortunately, they came to me while I was lying in bed that night, stewing over his smart aleck remark. Yes, Billy had managed to make a home run into a bad dream.

Well, Billy McMann is gone now, but some years ago Bull Derringer took his place. His dress, size, swagger, and age were different, but my gut reaction was the same. Only the commiseration of my fellow adults and my own sense of identity helped me deal more maturely with the situation his presence created. That situation, of course, was to beat the Bull at all costs.

## The Setup

One common phenomenon in baseball is that by mid-season, the children have taken on many of the adults' characteristics. If their coach bites his nails, half of them will do the same. If the manager calls the umpire a blind bum, the children will ridicule him as well, and blame him for every shortcoming they have. This has been proven time and time again. By mid-season, therefore, all of Bull Derringer's kids were like him—neat, fit, and swinging the bat like they had come out of the womb with it. And, like Derringer, they were all so sure of themselves, they were smart alecks, each and every one. Even kids I had coached as "Angels in Little League Clothing" had been changed into "Winning Robots" on his team, scoring runs in a methodical manner suggestive of the cocky 1987–88 season Mets.

Early Saturday morning, my tenth season as a coach, we were all to meet at the home of the league president to select our teams for the upcoming year. Having gotten up at five o'clock so I could finish rounds at the hospital and be at the meeting by eight o'clock, I was easily distracted by the permeating aromas of fresh-brewed coffee and cinnamon doughnuts. I was also relatively unprepared for the meeting, except for having some rough idea of the parents I wanted on my team, and a number of little notes stuffed in my pocket from parents asking me to please remember their child in the draft.

Bull, of course, had been the first one there, I was later told, arriving, as usual, with his two well-groomed coaches. Each had spread out his own notebook on the table before I had even arrived. As I sat down and reached for a doughnut, I noticed that only Bull was disciplined enough not to be stuffing himself with the free goodies.

The league president, a gentlemanly and kind-spoken man, tried setting an amiable atmosphere. He explained the purpose for the draft, which was to make sure all the teams would be of equal talent, so every child could feel he had a chance to compete and would feel good about himself.

We all listened intently, nodding our consent to the premise of fair play by equal and competitive teams. Within ten seconds of the draft opening, however, Bull had declared several of the president's suggestions unfair or illegal. The atmosphere quickly changed from amicable to something reminiscent of the showdown at the O.K. Corral. My hands perspired. My ego prodded, Don't let Bull buffalo you. Stand up to him. Tell him off, like all the other coaches wished they could. But my mind said no. I had been elected Manager of the Year. I would keep my perspective and self-control. I would act like an adult, not a child arguing over which half of the candy bar was bigger.

I quickly cut off Bull's interjections. "I want Bull to have all my first drafts. I'll take all the players he has on his least-wanted list." Everyone laughed—it was like a blast of fresh air. The guns were holstered and, except for a few skirmishes, the rest of the draft was uneventful. However, I was certain one gun was only loosely in its holster, ready to be fired the moment I turned my back. He was not known as The Derringer for nothing, I reasoned. Figuring I would beat him to the draw, therefore, I made the unfortunate move of not leaving my remarks at "I'll take all the players Bull has on his least-wanted list." Before he hit the ground from that first round into his chest, I followed it with another, well-aimed shot below the belt. "And when my little rejected kids beat you in the last game of the season, I will send them over to shake your hand." I got several real thumbs-up for that one from the other coaches. Bull merely showed me his superior, in-your-dreams smirk.

Actually, my Little League team turned out to be a good one. We handily won our first two games. Then the two undefeated teams—Bull's and mine—met. The other coaches wished me the best. "Kick his *bleep-bleep* off the field, Vince." Well, it was not even close. When the dust settled in the field, the score was Yankees 12, Orioles 6. I smile now. They had kicked our *bleep-bleep* off the field. Bull did not even come out to shake my hand. Not that he had it in for me, although I thought he did—he did not shake anyone's hand.

My little team went on to seven more losses in a row. Bull had not broken our spirit, just our train of thought. After all I had learned about attitude, about knowing one's self and keeping the game in perspective, the kids were still doing OK, but I was not. One more loss, and we would be in the cellar. Right then, we were just tied for it—the first time in my ten years of coaching I had not gotten my team into first or second place. Positive attitude comes easy when you are on top!

## The Game

As the practices went on, for the first time a number of players started not to show. Parental participation was also dwindling. Worst of all, my reputation as a come-from-behind coach was in jeopardy. If I continued to lose, who would buy my book? Maybe I could write a chapter, "Winning by Losing."

I feverishly looked at my schedule one Friday when I got home from the hospital. I knew I had to turn things around. I knew I could. I would be so positive, my enthusiasm would raise the players to a new level. I would give my players the "old gipper" talk. I would give my team parents the "old gipper" talk. I would give my coaching staff the "old gipper" talk—and the boot, if we did not win. I knew I could do it. I had done it hundreds of times before—or at least once or twice.

During my four years in high school, my baseball team was 0 and 79. I was captain of the team my senior year. As we went into the last game of the season, I swore to my teammates I would win this last one for them, since we had lost the first seventy-nine I had played in. Believe it or not, we won in the last inning of the eightieth game, 8–5. I will never forget it.

Recalling that spectacular comeback, I took a look at my Little League schedule. Oh, no! The Yankees! We had played them twice, and to say they had beaten us was an understatement— *slaughtered* was more like it.

Saturday, game day, was one of those "it feels good to be alive" days. As I walked out to the field, the grass was somehow brighter and more radiant than usual, its fragrance refreshing. We were playing on the major-league field, with its manicured infield and deep red-clay dirt. Somehow it inspired me.

My players were up, too, although still smoldering about "those damn Yankees." I quickly admonished the youngsters to respect their competitors, muttering only to myself, "Boy, those damn Yankees look good." I glanced quickly around—no one had heard that what I thought and what I said were not quite the same thing.

I decided to try a new tactic: no pep talk prior to the first inning. Instead of starting my first-string pitcher, I tried Conseco, who usually played third base. I saved my finest pitcher for last, as a possible comeback. Maybe I could lull the Yankees into complacency and then let the guillotine fall. The back of my mind said, "Who am I kidding?"

The game began. Strangely, Bull had put in his second-string pitcher. Generally, in the minors, each team has only two pitchers. At the most, you might occasionally find a third child that can throw the ball over the plate for a strike with any frequency.

Despite my best "gipper" talk at the beginning of the second, third, and fourth innings, and the parents being out in force to cheer on their little men and women, the score was 11–5 going into the fifth, and probably last, inning.

I was certain the Bull would now crush any resemblance of hope by putting in his "Ace," who rarely walked more than two or three batters a game; even the best pitchers in the minors average two to three walks per inning. But, surprise, no! The Yankees' third-stringer came in.

I tried rallying my Orioles. "Who are we?" I bellowed with half-hearted effort.

"The Birds," they yelled back, equally dejected.

The parents were busy discussing recipes and gazing at their watches, occasionally staring at them, as if trying to will the hands to move. Time sure flies when you are watching your kids get beat again. The first three batters in the top of the lineup walked, but instead of cheering on their teammates as they usually did, the children who were supposed to be in the dugout took off for left field, where they could pull off each other's hats and run around as if the game were already over. This gradually deteriorated into occasional outbursts. They knew, as I did, that Bull's Yankees might snuff us out anytime they wanted, simply by putting in the Ace.

In our minor league, even though only three walks were allowed, the player stayed up at bat until he got a hit or made an out. My big hitters the past six games had a total of ten hits among them—seven by one player, Big Mikey (formerly "Mighty Mike"), who I had just taken out to let one of the younger boys play, as a reward for his effort.

I did not let on that I knew the outcome, as I shouted once again, "Do we ever give up?"

"Never," my Birds called back as they briefly stopped their skirmishes on the side of the dugout.

I looked up in the stands and yelled, "Who here has a son that never gives up?" The parents momentarily looked up to acknowledge that I had ungraciously interrupted their conversations, then quickly went back to talking.

*Bang!* A good shot down the middle, two runs in, a man on first and third, and four runs to go.

I looked at Bull across the way, his arms nonchalantly folded, his eyes holding a steady, undaunted, and confident gaze. The next batter struck out. The following batter got up on an error, but our runner on third forgot he was on base and cheered his teammate to first instead of running.

The bases were loaded. My best batter was up. I knew Big Mikey was batting almost .700. I let my chest expand with hope. Let Bull put in the Ace; Mikey could hit anybody. Wait a minute— Alex was striding to the plate. I forgot I had taken out Big Mikey. Oh, how I hated myself. Sure, be generous, be good, do what is right, and you will always wind up like this, I thought. I shut my eyes and waited—not too long, mind you—as strike three was called.

Tony was up next. Potentially our best all-around player, he had not gotten a hit in three games. Then, it happened. Derringer made his move. He walked out to the mound and waved his arm. The Ace. We all knew. By this time, though, all my Birds were riveted to the game, cheering. They had even made up their own cheer, taken from the old Queen song: "We will, we will, rock you," followed by them all hitting the wooden dugout with their cleated shoes, *boom, boom.* It was ominous. Touchingly, even the parents forgot their small talk and stood to cheer in unison. The Yankees, for the first time, started to chant, too. I felt it. The whole thing had come down to me and the Bull. I knew it, and so did he. I could almost smell a faint aroma of cinnamon and fresh-brewed coffee from the day I had laid down the gauntlet. Yes, "it" was on the line—"it," spelled *p-r-i-d-e.* Bull motioned, and *he* came in. The Ace was not a very big player, so it was not easy to pick him out of all the other spotless, professional-looking Yanks.

As the young man tossed his first warm-up ball, I realized with a start that it was not the Ace—he was still in the field. Did the Bull feel that sure of himself?

The decision came quickly. *Blam!* Tony hit a hard drive over the center fielder to the fence. Three runs in, and Tony on third.

The Yankees catcher tossed the ball back to the new pitcher. Winding up, he launched one well over the catcher's head. Tony came striding in toward home plate. When he was no more than ten feet from home, the catcher grabbed the ball and dove toward him. Tony slid into the plate. The dust flew and the crowd went wild as the ump bellowed, "He's *safe!*"

Pandemonium broke out—12–11, what a beautiful score! We had won. All the boys on the field began hugging one another, the parents began hugging one another, and I nearly fainted. What a comeback! Suddenly, I got a sinking feeling in the pit of my stomach. I quickly glanced at my watch. We still had ten more minutes to play, officially. We had to stay alive for another ten minutes, or another inning would start, and all this jubilation, all my preaching about effort and how it always paid off in the end, might once again be snuffed out by the Bull. I had seen him do it a million times before—well, at least twice.

Brian, our next batter, quickly hit a grounder to first base. The inning was over, with eight minutes still left in the game. My heart sank. I motioned my players to get out to the field. The ump, too, checked his watch, and acknowledged the Dodgers and Giants, who were now in the bleachers waiting to take the field for their own game. The umpire motioned the coaches over. "There's still more than five minutes to go. Do you want to continue, Derringer?"

Bull Derringer turned to me. Our eyes met. I refused to let him see the disappointed uncertainty behind my facade of determination. A tiny smile began at the corner of his mouth, more like a sneer, I thought. Then he said, "It's been a good game. Let's call it."

For a second, the world as I knew it came to an abrupt halt. The children leaped into the air in slow motion and hung there in complete, dead silence as what had just occurred registered in my obstinate, judgmental, biased mind. Suddenly, the volume kicked back on, the cheer of "2-4-6-8" was over, and the kids headed toward one another to give their "nice game" handshake.

But it couldn't be! Bull was leading his troops. "Nice game," he smiled. "Great comeback, Orioles." He said it over and over, until my hand and his reached out for each other. He was wearing a genuine grin; I was so numb, I could not get up any smile at all.

I stammered, "My team may have won the game, but your team has, by far, the best coach." I thought I saw a trace of gratitude in Bull's face. He had truly won—I knew it and the ump knew it. As I sit here writing this, I want to make sure all the coaches who stayed around to offer encouragement to "beat the damn Yankees" know it, too.

## Life Is Full of Curveballs

After forty-five years, I thought I had it all figured out—but, obviously, I had not. We adults must keep our minds open, and recognize that it is often our own prejudiced attitudes that prevent others from being able to change. The memories and unresolved conflicts of our childhood are what cause our present and future to be just like our past—not the actual circumstances that we encounter. I learned a lesson that day I will not soon forget. This story is completely true, not made up or consolidated from several others to make a point. Little League in Pasadena, California, reached a new high that day, thanks to the Bull. Yes, I had met the enemy—and he truly was me!

# twenty-nine
## Darling's Disaster

### *Our trials are trivial when life is on the line*

I tossed and turned in bed, unable to get Don Darling and his Tigers out of my mind. I had the feeling that something was wrong, something potentially dangerous, but no one was paying attention to it, hoping it would go away by itself.

Don Darling had been managing Little League teams for eight years. Darling was a misnomer—Don was anything but. He was more like a disaster, at least to anyone who played him and his Tigers. I had heard he was a devoted coach. He got his team out to practice daily, which was good. What was bad was what he was teaching his youngsters.

All coaches try to teach their players to be assertive. Darling taught his Little Leaguers to be aggressive. The difference between assertive and aggressive is the difference between standing your own ground and knocking someone else over to take theirs. Darling's instructions demanded aggression: "When you slide into a bag, take 'em out. If they try to take home, make 'em pay." His mottoes were "Baseball is fifty percent talent, and one hundred percent guts," and "If they're afraid of you, they'll respect you." Don treated opposing coaches in the same manner, I had heard. I was looking forward to tomorrow's game like I would root-canal work.

I rubbed my eyes and grimaced. Eight-thirty A.M. Game time was 9:30 A.M. The sky was overcast when I reached the field, filled with steely gray clouds trapped against the San Gabriel Mountains. I herded my team into the dugout. Despite having gotten a rare full-night's sleep, my muscles felt tight and sore as I started running responses in my head to the inevitable confrontation with Mr. Darling. As I looked at my son and the other young faces of my team, I thought, Isn't Little League supposed to be enjoyable? Isn't it supposed to focus on these little boys and girls? I realized I was actually afraid—afraid of someone called, of all things, Mr. Darling; afraid of his players, and their reputation for roughness.

Two days earlier, I had seen Don and his catcher, nicknamed Grizzly because of the way he mauled anyone trying to steal home. Grizzly, or Brian Birksbye, was a big kid for eleven, who, it seemed, towered two feet over his opponents as they dared to approach home. Sliding into the plate with Grizzly behind it was like sliding into the mouth of a furnace, or even more, into the mouth of the giant shark in *Jaws*. The last game I saw him in, against the Yankees, Grizzly had stood in front of home plate like Goliath. As the Yankees runner turned third base to race toward home, Grizzly feigned that the ball was coming to him, and menacingly bellowed, "I'm going to knock your head off with this tag." The Yank hit the brakes and dashed back to third, only to bump into his teammate running from second. The ball, in fact, was just reaching second base at the time. Fear is contagious in little people; the Yankee's panic was quickly transmitted to his teammates. The runner coming from second ran back in terror, only to be tagged out. The runner who had been heading for home plate and was now back on third got confused by the shouts of his coach to go home, and started for home again, only now to be truly wasted by Grizzly's tag. Coach Darling dashed out to congratulate his catcher, who grunted, grinned a toothless grin, and pounded his chest. The parents of the Yanks stared in disbelief. The Yanks went out to the field with their heads slung low, already beaten by the Tigers. This is Little League baseball? I thought again. This is how we teach sportsmanship? How would I handle Darling and his monsters? In T-ball, it had been easy. Now, with ten-, eleven-, and twelve-year-olds, the game had taken on a new life. The children were more defiant, less easily controlled by adult intervention. Eleven marks the age of transition for many boys and girls, when parental influence begins to slip; when they get to thirteen, it does a complete nosedive. At the same time, their friends and idols—rock stars and the like—become all-important in the teenagers' eyes. Actually, it would not be so bad if the parents' influence simply slipped and flopped, but as soon as they become teenagers, our once adoring children begin to openly defy and occasionally berate the very people they used to call Mommy and Daddy. Why? Well, that is another book. I am going to call it *My Father's Revenge*.

## I Tried—Oh, How I Tried

Unless the coaches are in unison—unless there is a consistent example—children this age will be defiant, especially if led by an adult. Darling had only one thought: Win, even if you have to use force. I had heard him say it a dozen times. "These kids got to use the talents God gave them. If they are big, well, the big fish eat the little ones." Yes, yes, that is what a parent on his team told me. "The big fish eat the little ones." What was most startling about Darling was his stature: five-two and, at best, 120 pounds soaking wet. The psychiatrist in me came out. It was the "little man," or Napoleon Bonaparte syndrome (or, as one mother called it, PMS —Puny Male Syndrome). Darling was acting out his own wish to be a big man by intimidating others through his Little Leaguers, because all his life he had felt small. Now he was unconsciously getting even—you could see it in his eyes, and in his elation whenever Brian "Grizzly" Birksbye struck terror in the opposing players as they approached home plate.

I got to the ball field with time to spare. My team warmed up while their parents climbed into the stands, looking as if they were climbing into a dentist's chair. I could read the concern on some of the parents' faces as they eyed Grizzly, and then their little sons and daughters. The concern had washed away any hint of sparkle. In place of encouraging cheers, the moms and dads shouted warnings to be careful. Three parents came up to me and asked if I could do something to keep the game from getting out of hand.

Actually, I already had. My father had often told me, "Problems happen. What's important is how you deal with them." I had dealt with this one by calling Jack, the league president, the night before and explaining my dilemma. Well aware of the situation with Darling, he was more than happy with my solution. He joined me and the ump as I approached Don Darling, who was clutching his lineup board on the sidelines and yelling instructions to his Tigers. Don looked up to find us all converging on him.

I let the umpire start. He cleared his throat. "Look, there will be no intimidation permitted while I ump. Anyone who threatens or intimidates another player will be promptly thrown out of the game." Jack then added his own admonishments. Surprisingly, Darling's face did not show a single telltale reaction. He only smiled and said, "Certainly." As Jack and the ump left, I extended my hand in friendship to Don—and he unveiled the acrid rebuttal that had been hidden behind his friendly facade. "Chicken to play the Tigers, Vince? You've been in T-ball too long. You look like a big guy, but you're really a wimp. I thought they called your son 'Mighty.' I wonder where he got that name from—certainly not from you."

Me, a wimp? *Me!* Suddenly, I was shoved back through a time warp thirty-five years to the schoolyard and Penne, the most ornery, red-headed, freckle-faced, half-pint bully in the school. He had pushed me in front of my buddies, and in front of Grace, my secret sweetheart. "You're a chicken, Fatso," he had sneered in the demeaning voice only a bully can pull off.

Oh, how I regretted not knocking Penne into orbit! Oh, how did I ever say, "I can't fight you in the schoolyard because my mother would punish me."

"Oh, your mommy won't let you fight. You wimp. You chicken." I can still hear his nasally voice saying it over and over again. "You wimp. You wimp. You wimp." Oh, how I hated that word!

My little buddies had been disgusted with me; they gazed downward or off into space—anywhere away from me. All I could see of Gracie was her back as she walked away. I had been a head taller than Penne and twice as heavy—just as I was with Don Darling.

No, I told myself, I will not make the same mistake twice. That wimp image had haunted me ever since that fateful playground scene. As a young man, I had worked out this conflict by lifting weights, learning karate, and, finally, becoming a bouncer in college. It had not been enough just to be the bouncer at the Chop House, the most popular college bar; I had to get a job bouncing at the toughest bar in town, where no college student with any brains would go. I ended up having to fight every night, but did not quit until one of my fellow bouncers got shot to death. That must have awakened me, I guess. Now Darling was stirring up this sleeping giant again, but this time, I was no longer a kid. I was an adult, a respected medical professional, by God.

## When You Get to the End of Your Rope, Tie a Knot and Hang On

My anger grew to an internal fury, but all I said was "Get ready, Don, for a good game." Then, of course, I shook his hand hard enough to crunch his bones and make him wince in pain.

As I turned and walked away, I lectured myself: "Oh, Vince, don't let it get to you." My better judgment, though, told me I had done the right thing. Of course, knowing that did nothing to help loosen my tightly welded jaw or lower my skyrocketing blood pressure. My fists were clenched so tight, I could have crushed a piece of coal into a diamond. "Well," I consoled myself, "at least I didn't say my mother wouldn't let me fight."

I returned to the dugout, gathering up my team for a rousing "gipper" talk. "Fellas, the Tigers have a bad reputation, and a bad attitude. Today we are going to teach these bullies a lesson. The meaner they are, the nicer we'll be. When they see their threats don't scare, they'll stop using them. Then we'll show them that one good sportsman is worth a team full of bullies." I must have struck a chord in them, because when I gave them the cheer, "Who are we?" they answered with amazing gusto immediately, "The Cardinals!"

"Who are we?"

"Cardinals!"

"Who?"

"*Cardinals!*"

"Okay, get out there and paint 'em red."

Renato, one of my coaches, came over and slapped me on the back. "Great talk, Vince. 'Kill 'em with kindness.' I like that." Why is it our friends can see right through us?

I did not enjoy the type of game we played. Don had his players sliding into every bag with rubber cleats high. They taunted the Cardinals, but all my Birds held steady. Darling and his coaching staff continually egged their team on, calling to them, "Come on, be aggressive! Take 'em out! Drive it through 'em!" By the bottom of the sixth inning, the score was 3–3. My little guys were getting worn down by the Tiger jeers. Even worse, the team parents were getting ten sneers to every cheer they yelled. I took my team aside before they got up for the last inning.

"Okay, guys, they've given us their best, and the score is tied. Now let's show them what real baseball is all about."

I looked into the stands. The moms and dads were chewing their nails, probably praying for rain so they could just take their kids out of danger.

Two outs, a man on second and third. I was coaching third, where my runner, Luke Nakayama, stood. The Tigers' catcher, Grizzly, pointed at Luke. He did not have to speak a word—his sneer and menacing snarl said it all. Luke gulped, and his chin began to quiver. Luke was a dutiful, disciplined little boy with a loving family; his parents were at all his games. Honor and discipline were the mainstays of his heritage. I placed my hand on his shoulder and firmly told him not to be afraid of Grizzly. The umpire was in control. What slipped out of my mouth then I have regretted ever since. "Stand up to them, Luke. Be a man, or you'll regret it for the rest of your life." God, I cannot believe I said that. Thirty-five years later, knowing everything I did about psychiatry, I was still reliving my childhood.

Luke looked at me, then at Grizzly. He closed his eyes into slits, stuck his jaw out in defiance, and tightened his fists until his knuckles whitened. I could hear his parents say something in Japanese in the background. I did not know exactly what it was, but Luke's face became even more determined.

The pitcher threw a fast ball right down the center of the plate.

Kaycee smacked the ball dead center, hitting it into the hole between short and second base. The shortstop dove, deflecting the ball toward second with his glove. The second baseman picked it up and shot it toward Grizzly, who was covering—and blocking—home plate. Luke Nakayama, all three feet of him, slid right under Grizzly, but not in time to avoid getting Grizzly's gloved fist in the throat. Through the cheers and shouts and groans and cries, the ump bellowed, "You're safe!"

We all jumped off the bench in a frenzy, hugging and shouting. Over the din, Grizzly cried out in terror, "He's choking. He's choking!" Luke lay face up, clutching his throat. As we all rushed toward him, his lips began to turn blue, his eyes went up into his sockets, and his body became rigid and began to shake.

## Nothing Like a Good Dose of Reality

Luke was limp by the time I got to him. The rest of the fifty adults and twenty-five youngsters stood motionless, stunned, not knowing what to do. As I knelt by his side, my thousands of hours of medical training kicked in. I knew I had less than three minutes to do something, or little Luke, whom I had urged to "be a man," would be permanently brain damaged, or die. I checked his pulse by sliding my fingers alongside his tiny neck. His carotid bounded loudly. I then placed my ear over his mouth, but could feel no breath. Luke was not breathing! "Call the paramedics," I shouted. I tried mouth-to-mouth resuscitation repeatedly—unsuccessfully!

"Does anyone have a sharp knife?" Luke needed a tracheotomy, a hole through the front of his neck right below his Adam's apple, so he could breathe. I would have to be careful to avoid the thyroid gland full of blood vessels, or he would bleed to death.

The last tracheotomy I had performed had been in an emergency situation just after my internship as an emergency room doctor in Shirley, Long Island. That had been over twenty-three years ago.

It had now been more than a minute since the Little Leaguer had gone down. I had only another 120 seconds to do something or it might be too late. I called for a straw, to be used as a tube to be placed in the trachea—if, that is, I could find it, and get it open with a knife. I quickly picked Luke up, turned him upside down, and slapped him firmly between the shoulder blades five times. Nothing came out. I then thrust my fist just below his rib cage several times. Someone—it was Darling—held out a Swiss army knife, open to the razor-edged cutting blade. As I completed the third thrust, Luke suddenly let out a spew of air, along with a wad of pink gum. His little shoulders heaved as his grayish-blue body turned first white, then pink. He opened his eyes, and his mother and father suddenly came back to life. Sobbing feverishly, they hugged their baby, while the crowd went crazy, cheering and screaming with relief.

I slumped back on my heels, exhausted, relieved, shaken, I do not know what else. Looking up, I found Don standing with the handle of the knife still extended toward me. His eyes were glassy, his face still registering disbelief, horror, and guilt. Grizzly was sobbing in his dad's arms, "I didn't mean it. I didn't mean it." How ridiculous our conflicts seemed in that moment.

I stood up to meet Don's still stunned gaze. I was going to say, "Don, these are only children. We have to protect them so they can grow up to be men and women. This is just a game—something to play, something to bring happiness and adventure so they can look back with fond memories, and, hopefully, with experience they can use." But I did not speak a word. Don was obviously traumatized; his body language made it clear there was no lecture, no words of remonstration I could use that he was not already rebuking himself with. The true meaning of what we were doing out on the field had suddenly become so apparent to us all. Life is precious. Life is to be savored, not devoured. These were children, on a Little League baseball field, not soldiers on a battlefield. From that day forward, the Tigers were never feared again —their coach had realized the true meaning of the game.

## It's Baseball, Not Football

"I'm never going to allow my child to be subjected to this dangerous sport called Little League." If that is what you are now thinking, think again. In my and my fellow physicians' experience,

Little League is the safest of all sports. It has one-twentieth the injuries incurred by football, and one-tenth the ones incurred by soccer. Still, we adults must recognize what dangers do exist and make certain they are minimized. The biggest danger, and the one most important to confront, is any aggressive behavior that can harm the children physically or psychologically. We want our children to be assertive, not bullies. We want them to stand up for what is right and fair, not push for the extra advantage or win through intimidation and humiliation. If I have learned nothing else from my experiences on the ball field, I have learned that our children will adhere to whatever standards they see us follow— for good or evil. Whether we know it or not, we are always setting an example.

Every Little League parent and coach must know the fundamental safety rules of baseball, and insist on compliance:

- **No player should chew gum while playing,** as Luke did. Gum chewing is as dangerous for a major leaguer as it is for a Little Leaguer—it is, in fact, dangerous in any situation in which a person is engaged in physical activity, such as baseball, jogging, or even bike riding. If the gum is not lodged firmly between the teeth, it can be easily inspired into the windpipe any time a jolt, a yell, or even the anticipation of something exciting causes a forcible inward breath.
- **Little League coaches and managers must learn life-support techniques,** not only for children, but even for the parents and grandparents who attend the games.
- **No child should be allowed to swing a bat without supervision.** Unattended bat swinging actually causes most of the more serious injuries in children's baseball. Collect all the bats, even those the children bring to the game, or give each child's bat to the parent to hold when it is not his turn at the plate. No child should be permitted to carry the bat home with him unless it is placed in his game bag. Many children get hurt in the parking lot when

a child, dreaming of hitting a home run, swings the bat inadvertently into the nearby head of another child.

Coaches must recognize the real purpose of Little League is to give children a positive experience that encourages them to keep trying, and to work toward gaining those important ingredients they will need as adults—effort, consistency, discipline, and empathy. They, as well as the team parents and managers, need to realize that the Little League diamond is not a field for working out adult unresolved conflicts, setting right childhood mishaps, or proving macho worth. The Little League field is for *children to have fun.*

# thirty

## Coaching the Last-Place Team

*It's not over till it's over*

*—Yogi Berra*

I never intended to write this chapter. I never had a losing team. Then, in my eleventh season, I did—and I learned the real difference between being positive when you are winning and being positive when you are at the bottom of the heap.

The sun was setting. The third baseman, Saji, had beads of perspiration dripping from his furrowed little forehead. His jersey was so drenched it could not hold any more perspiration. The catcher, Andrew, gave the sign to Brent out on the pitcher's mound. Rearing back, Brent launched another strike-zone throw to the plate. The crack of the bat on the ball resonated in my empty skull cavity as my eyes tracked yet another shot through the shortstop's legs, past the left fielder, and all the way to the outfield fence. One run, two runs, three runs. I screamed, "Third, third, third," as the ball was thrown past the second baseman, got bobbled by the pitcher, and was finally hurled into the stands just as the fourth run crossed the plate.

Ecstasy for the Giants—they jumped all over, giving each other high fives, low fives, and inside-out fives.

In contrast, my team's small shoulders were slumping, their eyes drooping and cast to the ground. The score was into double figures already, with only one man out in the first inning. Custer's Last Stand was near-victory compared with this massacre. At least Custer did not have any survivors to remind him of what had happened.

I glanced at my team parents. One mother's fist was clinched in anguish; another was absentmindedly wringing her hands as if she were washing them of this inning. Mama Maria's rosary was thoroughly worn out. Only grimaces, not grins, showed on their faces as another screaming line drive darted through our Orioles, who kept to their positions even though each hit brought their chins a little closer to the ground.

Toward the end of the third inning, the ultimate insult was cast in our faces. The Giants' coach smugly called out, "Jimmy, we have to complete three innings, or the game will be incomplete." Jimmy proceeded to deliberately hit a dribbler to first, then proudly trotted to the base like a rooster crossing the chicken coop.

Twenty-seven to two. My enthusiasm was paper thin. What could I do, pray for rain? Even better, maybe a small earthquake would erupt—nothing dangerous, just enough to call the game. Hey, it had worked in the World Series when the Athletics played the Giants. As the game plummeted to a close, I tried to round up my Birds.

"Two, four, six, eight, who do we appreciate? Giants! Giants!" echoed across the field, but I was the only Oriole hearing it. My team parents and children had all evaporated, rather than walked off the field. I stared at the vacant diamond, the distant chatter of the boisterous victors moving away toward their cars. Taking a deep breath, I lugged the field bag off to my own van. Alone, so alone! Contentment breeds success, I had always preached. Hogwash!

This had been the twelfth defeat in the past fourteen games of the season; we had won our first two times out. The Giants were the only team near enough in the standings to be seen with us on the same page. One more loss, and our team name might drop off the end of the weekly Little League newsletter.

I lay awake in bed that night long enough for my wife, Arlene, to notice. "What's wrong, worried about a patient? Someone threatening to sue you?"

"It's much worse than any of that," I moaned. "I'm a loser. I can't help my little team. You had to be there, it was terrible."

"I was there," Arlene reminded me. "You know, they really aren't as bad as they look." I groaned.

"Well, I know what I could do," I said to myself. "I'll show them what I've been writing really works!"

Have you ever just finished telling your buddies how you kicked the heck out of the local bully, only to turn around and find him standing behind you? Now your fantasy is facing reality, as the blood drains out of your face. That week, I called all the parents personally: "Hello, Mr. McGinnis, this is Sean's coach. What did you say? 'When is your child going to win?' That's what I'm calling about. Winning and losing are only a matter of attitude. Did you know that learning how to lose can actually be more important than winning? Let me explain."

Mr. McGinnis listened intently, or maybe just fell asleep. I hoped what I told him would make a difference, as his son, Sean, had the bad habit of saying what everyone else was thinking— especially when I was trying to make them forget it.

Besides all the phone calls, I went to great lengths to make that week's practices especially inspiring. I must have bellowed "nice play," "nice hit," and especially "nice try" a thousand times. I even made new signs to put up in preparation for our weekend game, which was against the devastating Dodgers, of all teams. Their uniforms seemed especially bright that day, the sunlight gleaming off them as if they were polished armor. They all looked as if they had grown a foot in the past two weeks, compared with my Birds.

"Everybody in the dugout," I called. I had gone over my speech several times as I drove to the field. The Gettysburg Address was mere humdrum compared with this inspirational monologue. I started with reality. "Well, team, we've had a tough time. But tough is what we're all about, isn't it?" I raised my voice two or three octaves, my usual cue for my tots to bellow, "Right, Coach!"

And they enthusiastically did—sort of.

"The Dodgers are a good, tough team, but we are . . ."

"Better," they obediently chimed.

I then launched into my absolutely most inspiring gipper talk. It even got my own adrenaline pumping. As I ended, each little face gleamed. Pausing, I could see a raised hand out of the corner of my eye. "Yes, Sean?"

With a high-pitched sneer he said, "Who are you kiddin', Coach, they're gonna kill us again." Eleven little heads nodded in unison. Abraham Lincoln had his John Wilkes Booth—I had my Sean Edward McGinnis.

## Losing Is Only an Attitude

The score was 6–7 going into the next-to-last inning—the first time in eight games the other team had fewer runs earned than a marathon has miles. For once, the official scorekeeper had not gotten bewildered trying to figure out how to show double figures in one inning on the scoreboard out in right field. Did you know that the numbers for those little boxes only go from one to nine? If a team scores ten runs or more in one inning, it cannot be put up. No one had ever needed to think of that eventuality, until my Birds flew to the Little League field.

Despite McGinnis shocking us all back into reality, my call to the parents had worked. The stands thundered with enthusiasm. Mama Maria's rosaries were left at home under orders (though she informed me she had said several decades prior to the game). Wringing hands and clenched fists were changed into applause and chants: "Let's go, Orioles, let's go! *Boom! Boom!*" Their stomps on the dilapidated wooden stands resounded across the field. The incessant chorus was as daunting as it was enchanting. At the end of the second inning, the umpire warned me, "The opposing coach says you're intimidating his kids."

I looked up in dismay. "I didn't mean anything negative toward his children. I was only urging my little guys on."

The umpire winked. "I knew, and I told him that myself. Keep it up, and you might just beat this rowdy bunch."

Okay—we were down by one run and up to bat. Ball four—I had never heard such sweet words. Andrew, our fastest runner, trotted to first. Strike three, a number I had never before realized I could detest so severely. I knew winning was not the reason for playing the game—I had pounded that into the parents' heads all week. We were there to see the children grow, to show unconditional love to all the players, even if they lost.

"I know losing is never fatal," I prayed. "But, Lord, winning once in a while instills confidence and repetition of positive behavior, too." Andrew streaked to second, safe by a mile.

James was up next. I gave him a pep talk, and reminded him to swing only at those balls that were between his knees and chest. James, all three feet of him, had the habit of thinking he was six feet tall, like his dad. Even with the bat extended over his head, he could not make five feet. Henry, the Dodgers' pitcher, went into his windup and lofted one six feet high; James went amnesiac and swung. Strike one!

"Nice swing," I croaked out with as much enthusiasm as possible. "Remember now to swing at one over the plate."

The next pitch bounced into the dirt. Using a golf swing, James shot the ball past the pitcher. Unfortunately, it was cut off by the shortstop, but what James lacked in pitching selection, he made up for in speed.

Runners on first and third, one out. Brian, the bottom-of-the-bottom of our lineup, strode to the plate. Measuring out his distance with the bat, he stood three feet from the plate—a small precaution, he had previously told me, in case of a wild pitch. The Orioles' parents were in a frenzy. "Let's go, Brian, let's go! *Boom! Boom!*"

Brian was 0 and 21 for the year but had walked several times. Mama Maria started praying. Andrew inched off third by four or five yards, despite my pleading with him to get closer to the base so he would not be picked off. James darted for second as the first ball was pitched. *Clang!*—a sound so previously nauseating now resounded like the clash of cymbals as an inside pitch sped off Brian's bat over the outstretched hand of the first baseman. One run, 7–7. Around came James as the right fielder gathered up the ball and started his throw to home. The reverberation from both sides of the stands was deafening. The ball slammed into the catcher's mitt just as James slid into home. A momentary hush, then, "Safe!" The crowd exploded.

All the Orioles sprang from the bench to whoop around Brian. His gleaming smile could have lit up a moonless desert night for a week. This is what Little League is all about, I thought happily. This is what makes all the time, aggravation, and work worthwhile.

Something had happened that evening—to the team, and to the parents. The players had never had much talent, but that game, they found something that transcended any inadequacy in throwing, batting, or fielding: they found heart, just like the "Damn Yankees" song said they "gotta have." Heart gave them hope and opened them to the concept of "try and you will succeed." Yes, it was true: each and every one of those Little Leaguers was a winner no matter what the score—8–7, or 100–7!

# thirty-one

## The Team That "Got It"

***Life is a marathon, not a series of fifty-yard dashes***

My eleventh season came to a close with a record sixteen losses, four wins, and one tie. The last five games were more rewarding than any other I have ever coached. After our win from the Dodgers, I tried to maintain the positive attitude that had lit up my Birds, as they had been nicknamed in the league (as in "For the . . ." the joke went).

We lost our next game in the last inning to the Expos, a formidable team, but, I told myself, it had only been a warm-up for the following, more important encounter with the Giants, who were only one game ahead of the last-place team—us! The beating they had given us earlier would have been long forgotten but for their coach's bad habit of constantly reminding them about "that great win against the Birds—twenty-seven to two." We played them the second to last game of the season.

### One for the Books

To warm up, my little Birds were having fun playing the games I had taught them, which, in actuality, were designed to sharpen their fundamental baseball skills. Winning seemed far from their minds. They were just there to have fun. Finally, ten minutes late as usual, the umpire called, "Ball in!"

I rounded up my team, stood especially tall before them, and placed my hands on my hips. "Well, fellas, this is a good team we are playing. No matter how many runs they score, will we give up?"

"No way, Coach."

"Who are we?"

"Orioles, Orioles! *Orioles!*"

"Well, then, let's go out there and have a great time!" I did not voice my conscious thought, Let's win.

Suddenly, as always, McGinnis raised his hand. "Let's beat these guys, they said we stink! Larry, their pitcher, told me yesterday in the schoolyard we're for the birds."

I immediately went back to the lineup and scratched in McGinnis to start the game. Nothing like a little positive incentive for constructive criticism, I thought.

It was a long and exciting game. Bottom of the fourth, and definitely last, inning. Our right attitude, adulatory parents, and recent win/near-win streak had paid off. As the sun sat over the horizon, the score was 3–15. That's right—all we had to do was hold them scoreless, rack up thirteen runs ourselves, and we had the game locked up!

Sean McGinnis, the closest thing I have ever seen to a leprechaun, was up first. I had kept him in the whole game. I even had him catching the last inning—something he had pleaded for all year. The Giants had been unmerciful, with Larry, their pitcher, laughing and ridiculing my Birds the most. McGinnis had tried with all his heart to hit Larry's pitches, but he could succeed only in striking out.

As Sean stood just outside the batter's box, I placed my arm over his slumped shoulder. "Do we ever give up?" I whispered in his ear.

"I don't know," he said, shaking his head no.

"Imagine hitting a line drive right over Larry's freckled head. Remember, Sean, he expects you to swing at his first pitch, so wait till the third one." Sean walked up to the plate. Ball one. Ball two. On the third pitch, Sean reared back to swing, and the ball hit him in the arm. Gritting his teeth and straining to keep back his tears, he held his hand over his tiny biceps and rubbed. No way was his friend Larry going to see him cry. Sean trotted to first, staring at the pitcher, but he did not stop there. As soon as he rounded first, he immediately took off for second.

"No!" I yelled, but Larry was so stunned at this brazen act, his throw went over the second baseman's head—and Sean was on third.

No outs, man on third, and twelve runs to tie, thirteen to win. Improbable? Yes. Impossible? No. What happened next must surely go down in the annals of Little League history. For once, the Birds were the ones who caused the scorekeeper trouble with placing double digits on the scoreboard. Maybe all my motivational techniques had caught up to them—or maybe they had been inspired by Sean's boldness. Whatever the reason, they just kept hitting the ball and pulling in the runs.

Second and third, two outs, eleven runs. Mighty Mike, my most reliable hitter, was up—and he was ready. The Giants' stands were silent. Larry had long ago been taken out as the game extended into the second half of the hour. The opposing coach was loudly complaining, "My players can't see."

The ump only laughed. "Seems the batters aren't having any problems."

The Giants' pitcher went into his windup and threw. The ball was two feet too high, and a foot outside, but that did not stop Mikey—he hammered it down the right-field line. One run across! The game was tied. I could not hear my own shouts over the noise from the stands as hefty Mike lumbered around first base. The Giants' first-base coach ran out toward right field, barking, "Throw it to home, throw it to home!"

It was the fastest relay I have ever seen. The right fielder paid no attention whatsoever to his imploring coach and threw the ball to second. Mikey, counting his chickens before they had hatched, was skipping to second, totally unaware of the throw. The ump bellowed, "You're out!" just one beat before the thirteenth run crossed over the plate, and two seconds before the sun set. The parents on both sides were wildly jubilant. Victory was snatched from the jaws of defeat—but for whom? It was the ultimate Little League victory—both sides had won.

Since it was too dark to play another inning, the ump declared the game over. As I meandered off the field, I was overwhelmed by the wonder of it all. Had I been wrong about their talent? No, I had been around for too long to have been mistaken about that. Then why had it happened to set my last-place team on a winning streak? The only answer I could come up with was that the parents had finally begun to believe in their children, which sparked the players' belief in themselves. What else could explain it?

In the last game of the season, the Birds were up against the Twins, who needed this win to make the playoffs for the league championship. I can only sum it up as a 17–8 slaughter. The Orioles made nineteen hits in five innings, scoring a total of twenty-nine runs in six innings—which was about as many as they had previously scored all season. Why?

I have talked of focus, timing, and encouragement. Despite all my platitudes, one coach once told me, "You can say what you want, but if your team doesn't win, your kids will walk away losers." When my team was 2 and 12, that statement haunted me. Baseball is only a small part of my life. I work a minimum of twelve hours daily with patients whose lives occasionally hang on my decisions. I lecture physicians, and I am involved in the bioethics of medicine. Little League baseball, however, is a focal point in my life—a testing ground for ultimate truth and success. I may touch many people's lives in medicine, but I still feel a void. Millions of little lives are affected yearly in Little League—unfortunately, for many, that effect is negative. I have yet to speak to a parent whose child has not had several bad experiences in Little League. I believe this can be changed. The "Bad News Bears" image so many Americans identify Little League with can be changed to the Good News Cubs—or Padres, or Birds, or Dodgers.

## The Recipe of Encouragement

Before I "got it," my eleventh season team was 2 and 12. One of those wins was a forfeit, the other a 6–5 surprise. The other teams were maturing, and the children who already had potential were rapidly gaining confidence as their skills improved and their teams won. I had given it some thought. Confidence comes from skills and winning, but does one need both, or just one of the two? And which comes first? With my schedule at work, I knew I could not possibly increase the number of practices. My co-coach, a deeply dedicated father and friend, was born in Brazil and knew a lot about soccer but little about baseball. I wrote down my problem: "How can I improve their skills and, at the same time, reinforce their efforts with positive feedback, since it is unlikely I can give them the reinforcement of winning a game?"

I thought about the concept of reflected self-image: a child assesses himself on how his parents or an adult surrogate, in this case the coach, regards his performance. Well, I could certainly reflect a positive image to the children, and see to it that the other coaches and parents did, too. Creating a positive environment where the children could grow at their own rate was another thing.

How could I increase what seemed to be the all-important ingredient—their confidence? No matter how easily I attempted to pitch during practice, some children missed the ball more often than not, while others did fairly well. They all did OK playing the field in practice but faltered during the actual game. After long reflection, I decided I needed to drastically change the practices. One thing my Birds could do was fly—that is, run. I instituted three new things: practice forms that would show them they could succeed, constant reinforcement of that concept, and training sessions that were more fun than drill.

If you have been at standard Little League practices, you know that everybody takes their positions while the coach hits the ball to the infielders. They throw it around to first base, then practice double plays. All the while the coach yells, "Bend your knees, keep your glove down, keep your eye on the ball." Meanwhile, you can catch the outfielders feeling like second-rate citizens and falling asleep. Obviously, all this had to change.

I started with batting. I taught them bunting and pepper. In ten minutes, they had caught on, and I could place one batter against three fielders. The fielders lobbed the ball from ten feet away to the batter, who bunted. All the players learned quickly and had a high rate of success. I played especially with the least-talented children, giving them the extra help they needed. In these little groups, I could also get more parents involved. Parents become amazingly understanding when they are part of the coaching staff. One rule, though: never let a parent coach his or her own child at practice.

Next, I divided my Birds into three groups of four equal-talent players. We played "catcher up." One child would throw fly balls, and the other three would try to catch them. Three catches, and you could throw the ball. In two practices, I accomplished more with many of my players than I had in the entire previous seven weeks.

We then went on to infield practice, but with a twist. I had the usual outfielders put on helmets and act as runners. This gave the infielders the chance to practice under game conditions. At the same time, the usually less talented children, who played outfield, learned the strategies of running, leading off, and sliding. Finally, at the end of the practice, we had our base-running race. Each child kept track of his own times, both to first base and around all the bags. The parents cheered them on.

With a little "creative timing," each child improved over each practice. Some of them really improved. Those who had formerly felt clumsy were most affected by this, as they tried harder than ever to beat their own previous best.

By the third practice, a miracle had occurred. Everyone arrived on time to practice, and, even better, though the sessions started going beyond the allotted hour, no one complained of being tired anymore. As an added reward for their great efforts, I would take them to McDonald's for a burger. The traditional practice was gone. Each child had been grouped with other children who had similar talent, so they could all enjoy themselves and succeed. As they succeeded, they tried harder. Practice became fun, a game. Even the coaches and parents had fun seeing the children so happy, which made our enthusiasm at the games real, and carried the spirit right back to the children.

The team that did not have it, got it. No, we did not have the raw talent of the other teams, but what we had now was something more important. The children were having fun and were not afraid of losing. Their parents were proud of them, and they were proud of themselves. The true ingredients of a Little League team had been sown: camaraderie, fun, discipline, contentment, and increasing effort. Put them all together, and they grow confidence.

## I Grew Up

As I look at Little League in retrospect, I think of my now twenty-year-old son, Vinny—the "Bionic Man" at six. Little League was only a small, albeit important part of his development. When I first entered the game I would dash to the field. Each pitch, each ball hit to him, had me sitting at the edge of my chair. I was overwhelmed with emotion at each little event. This often made me place incredible expectations on my son, and agonize over things I now see as utterly trivial. I am sure I was only hurting him as he read my disappointed and angry facial expressions. I see things so much clearer now. Little League is just one of the miles of the marathon of life. The most important part of it is making sure our children have a wonderful experience that teaches them to try, and to be content with their effort and themselves.

We, as parents, must put Little League in the right perspective and not get lost in the moment. We must remember that we teach our children through our actions and facial expressions. We must demonstrate behavior and advice to our children that encourages repeated effort, knowing that effort will eventually bring discipline. We must give the encouragement that breeds contentment. Little League can—and should—be exhilarating and fun. For me, it has been a twelve-year trek through one of the most beautiful parks in the world, where jewels have sparkled and lit up my life like no other diamond ever could.

Yes, Little League is alive and well in Pasadena, California. The number of children participating has grown by 40 percent since my fourth year in the league. People are learning that the family that plays together, grows together. The Great American Pastime is no longer an endangered species. As you close this book, call your child and take him, or her, to a ball game. My wish is for you to know the same pleasure I enjoy whenever my daughter, Kaycee, says, "Dad, every time I pass a baseball field, I just feel good all over!"

Ah, baseball! I love it!

# EPILOGUE: Whatever Happened to Those Little Leaguers?

Vinny, the "Bionic Man," who played the bench in Little League majors and had a tough time grabbing a ball dropped into his glove, no less catching one thrown from forty-five feet away, went on to be named MVP on his high school varsity tennis team and was enlisted into his high school's Hall of Fame for outstanding tennis record.

Charlie, who had difficulty throwing a baseball within ten feet of first base when he was playing second base, only thirty feet away, was named Basketball MVP in grammar school. Averaging eighteen points a game and the most rebounds, he was sought after by several high school basketball teams. Charlie never gave up, because his parents never gave up.

Greg, who "should not be allowed to continue in Little League . . . it's too dangerous for him," was voted most popular in his class, and currently has a ten handicap in golf. His dad had been correct—he could not change the color of his son's eyes, only the sparkle in them. Greg is proof positive that character takes one farther than talent.

Mary, one of the three girls on my first team, and the one my dad recognized we could not do without, went on to play softball in high school. I see her every now and again in one of the hospitals I work at. She is a nurse—the very kind no hospital can do without!

Tony, the five-errors-in-one-play kid, is the first-string pitcher for his high school team, a lefty with the potential to become a major leaguer. He has no recollection whatsoever of making those five errors, because no one ever ground them into his memory.

Everett, lanky, long-nosed, and awkward, won a scholarship for college in track, where his skills are appreciated. He remembers being made fun of, and it still hurts him, but, he says, "I'm over it." Some scars do not show on the outside; we can only guess how much they ache on the inside as time goes on. Some people, like Everett, are empowered by these hurts to succeed despite all the odds. As coaches, we have an obligation to make Little League a harmonious place in which to grow.

Tucker Cox, the most talented fielder in the league, dropped out of sports in his senior year of high school. His dad, the infamous Coach Cox, still cannot understand why.

Patrick, Tri's son, who was a fine player one moment and a zombie the next, is doing well at UCLA now. When he thinks back to his Little League days, he smiles and says, "Ah, the Padres." He does not recall his zombie routine—he only remembers the first double play he made at shortstop. It is a good thing his father and I made that deal.

Andy, whose arms were so frail they could barely support the weight of the bat, and whose father was prepared to take him out of competitive sports because he was too small, is now fifteen years old, six feet tall, and by no stretch of the imagination frail. Each child physically matures at a different age. Never compare your children with others physically; just nurture their minds and egos, and soon enough their bodies will come along. What will see them through life is not their size or talent, but their character.

I saw Sammy, the boy who cried when hit by a soft grounder and pointed to his heart to show where it hurt, as a patient when he was a teenager. He was having tension headaches. His mother noticed he got them every time he had an important exam coming up. I had no doubt that his father-coach, who had sarcastically said, "This kid is a crybaby," was intensely involved, trying his best to help and teach Sammy. Unfortunately, he expected too much from the boy, both in Little League and in his teen years, and, despite his good intentions, managed only to crush rather than nurture him.

Chad, the indecisive boy with the inconsistent parents, went to live with his grandparents when his folks got divorced. I am told he is doing well.

Stefan, part of the "iron curtain" infield, was the MVP in baseball, soccer, and whatever else he touched. When he got to college, he found himself faced with a negative coach who could not accept himself and projected all his problems onto the ballplayers. Stefan had character besides talent, though, so he transferred schools, and went on. He recognized that his self-worth did not depend on a coach's or anyone else's evaluation of him. He was made of the right stuff. When faced with a brick wall, do not continue to bang your head against it; find a way around it, and keep going forward.

Kaycee, the "Be nice or you're off the team" girl, suffered from encephalitis. She was paralyzed for one week on her right side and unable to talk. Subsequently, she also suffered from epilepsy. Several years later, at age fourteen, she was awarded Grand National Karate Championship for Red Dragon Karate, repeating the feat the following year. She was the first girl to ever be Grand Champion, and the first person—man or woman—to ever win it twice. Currently, she is in college. She is the epitome of "Where there is a will, there is a way."

Mr. Burnham's son, Brandon, turned out to be a lonely young man. He was sent to a private school out of the country, and, the last I heard, was studying pre-law in college.

Willard's parents became managers of a minor league team the year after he played on mine, with the English-accented Mr. Burnham as a coach. They were therapeutic for one another. They played my team, and Willard pitched against us. I will let you guess the outcome.

Reggie, whose dad thought checking out the local Dodge dealer was more important than watching his son practice, graduated from high school with high honors. His mother was as proud as a peacock. His dad, Reginald, could not attend, as he had an important meeting. Reggie publicly hugged and thanked his mom for all she had done for him, and for helping him to be all he could be. He never mentioned his father, who, I am told, is still looking for the car of his dreams. Some day he may wake up and realize he is alone, but I will bet he will not know why.

Clark, the Overachiever bred by Overachiever parents, whose mother had promised him a bike if he hit a home run, grew up to be everything his parents wanted: a lawyer at the best firm in the state. Unfortunately, he was unable to sufficiently please his boss fast enough for what was "expected." When told he would not be asked to be a partner, he went back to his office and ended his life with a single bullet. No one could figure out why. He had it all —except, of course, self-acceptance. He depended on others to accept him, and when they did not, he could not bear it. His life was successful in all the outward ways, but the price for that status was unbearable. I only wish his parents—especially his mom—had taken Little League's learning more to heart: there is more to success than winning.

You can prevent history from repeating itself. You have a great influence on your children during their Little League years. Know yourself, accept yourself, love yourself, and your child will grow up contented and self-reliant. *Remember: character, not talent, determines your child's—and your—destiny.*

# Appendix A:
# The History of
# Baseball

Baseball is believed to have been founded in England in the 1600s. Originally, the game had three bases, and the idea was to hit the ball with the bat. Each base was actually a stake driven into the ground, some three feet high. Fielders put their base runners out by hitting them as they dashed to the base with the thrown ball. This was known as "plugging the runner."

English settlers brought this bat-and-ball game with them to America. By the 1700s, it had begun its evolution into One Old Cat, Two Old Cat, and then, simply, Town Ball. One Old Cat used only one base and required three players: a pitcher, a catcher, and a batter. As the game became more sophisticated, two more bases were added, along with additional players.

*A Little Pretty Pocket Book*, first published in 1744, gives us an example of early baseball, and clearly states its purpose—enjoyment.

> "the ball once struck off
> away flies the boy
> to the next destined point,
> and then home with joy."

As you might imagine, the stakes or posts banged into the ground were neither fun to run into, nor very practical. They were soon replaced with flat stones—and it does not take too much imagination to picture the injuries those, too, could inflict. Finally, sacks filled with sand became the precursors of today's bases.

Logic (and, I am certain, many a large welt) caused plugging the player to be changed into tagging the runner. Originally, all runners had to be tagged out. Eventually, due to frequent collisions at the bases—especially first—that rule was finally changed. The new rule said that a defensive player only had to touch the bag to score the out if a player was running from one base to another. To be fair, the rules said, the player who had just hit the ball could run past the bag on first base without being penalized or tagged out as he returned to the base. Even before the rules of the game were formally written, these and other common-sense safety rules evolved over the course of time.

Abner Doubleday, legend has it, created the contemporary game of baseball in Cooperstown, a small village in New York. Cooperstown now houses the Baseball Hall of Fame. A general in the U.S. Army, Doubleday is believed to have popularized the game in central New York. Although he may not have been the one who actually invented baseball, he is definitely responsible for its widespread popularity.

Alexander J. Cartwright, founder of the Knickerbocker Base Ball Club of New York, apparently wrote down the first set of rules for the game. He established the distance of ninety feet between bases, the standard of nine positions on the field, and the difference between fair and foul territory.

On June 19, 1846, the Knickerbocker Club played the New York Nine at Elysian Field in Hoboken, New Jersey, in what is historically considered the first official baseball game. During the Civil War (1861 to 1865), New England Union soldiers spread their love of the game throughout the states. In 1876, William Hulbert, owner of the Chicago White Stockings, formed the National League. Its first league game, between Boston and Philadelphia, was played on April 27, 1876, with more than three thousand in attendance. In 1901, the American League was born, setting the stage for the World Series to evolve.

Baseball continued to spread in popularity through the newspapers and, finally, the radio. The first radio broadcast of a game took place on August 25, 1921, when station KDKA in Pittsburgh transmitted a play-by-play account of the contest between the Pirates and Philadelphia Phillies. On August 26, 1939, baseball first appeared on television over station W2XBS.

The first baseball gloves did not make their appearance until 1875. Originally, the players played bare-handed and used bats borrowed from cricket. Cricket "bats" are actually short, flat-sided poles. Round bats were introduced to baseball in 1862. At first, when they were made of white ash, the best bat wood was found in the forests of Pennsylvania and northern New York. However, due to the concern over bats breaking or splintering and causing injury, aluminum bats made their appearance in the late 1960s and early 1970s. At one time, more than 10 million wooden bats were made a year. With the low cost of aluminum bats today, only a million or less wooden ones are now made per year. Aluminum bats are still not used in the majors, though, because they would cause big changes in the game, and possibly wipe out many hitting records.

Uniforms were first introduced by the New York Knickerbockers in approximately 1851. They included long, dark-blue trousers, webbed belts, white shirts, and straw hats. At first the uniforms were very baggy, but, in a style pioneered by Willie Mays in the early 1960s, they have since become more close-fitting. The Pittsburgh Pirates wore the first batting helmets on September 15, 1952, using them not only at bat, but in the field as well. After a few years, the Pirates decided their players needed to wear the helmets only on trips to the plate.

The early helmets had no earflaps. Earflaps were actually developed for Little League play, and copied later by the major leagues. I remember well the first year helmets were introduced to Little League on Long Island—1953—because it was the year I began to pitch. Luckily for three players, our helmets had earflaps. I still question the policy of not having T-ballers wear helmets on the field.

## A Part of History

Helmets always remind me of Andrew. We were playing an evening game, the third game of the season, and not many of the parents had shown up, for one reason or another. Andrew was up at the plate with his helmet on. He hit the ball off the tee and dashed toward first. He grinned as the first-base coach told him to head toward second. The right fielder picked up the ball, ran after Andrew as he turned first, and threw it at his back, hitting instead the back of Andrew's head. He must have gotten confused and thought we still "plugged" our runners, rather than tagged them out. Luckily, Andrew was wearing his helmet. After the play, the umpire gently admonished the right fielder, who truly had not recognized his error. The inning was soon over, and the Blue Jays were up to bat.

Andrew, who was then in his first year of Little League, ran out with all his teammates, to play left field. The Blue Jays put a man on first and second. One of their bigger players smashed a line drive into the outfield. Little Andrew dashed headlong toward the ball with his arm extended, only to catch it squarely on his forehead. His legs flew out from under him, and he landed on his back. I dashed for left field. Our shortstop, Mary, however, alert as usual, caught the ball on the bounce off Andrew's head, turned, and tagged the base runner out as he rounded second for third. When I arrived at Andrew's side, he was just picking up his helmet. He had forgotten to take it off to play the field! I looked at his head—not a mark. The helmet had protected him.

For the rest of the year, I had all the outfielders wear helmets until I was certain they could catch the ball safely. Perhaps the Pirates were correct by having their players use the helmets out in the field. While it may be awkward for the infielders, it is an added safety measure for those children with poor catching skills. I feel coaches should have the prerogative to use and be supplied with any equipment that will protect their Little Leaguers.

Andrew was actually lucky twice: first, that he had his helmet on to protect him from possible injury and a potentially bad experience that might have made him ball-shy (and robbed us of our eventual star catcher); and second, that the dugout Mom had not shown up that day. She probably would have reminded him to take off his helmet and put on his hat!

# Appendix B:
# The History of
# Little League

1939

In Europe, Hitler's armies marched into Czechoslovakia, marking the start of World War II. In America, the Great Depression tapered to an end, bringing forth a new sense of vitality, strength, and optimism to every fiber of American society. In Hollywood, *Gone With the Wind* and *The Wizard of Oz* exploded onto the silver screen, delighting moviegoers across the country. In Cooperstown, New York, the Baseball Hall of Fame opened, compensating only somewhat for Lou Gehrig's "Farewell to Baseball" speech.

Another momentous event occurred that year, one that would have far-reaching effects for millions of children and adults. It did not make the front page or the radio newscasts, but like a small seedling peeking its head up through the hard ground, it changed the face of America, eventually becoming more important, in a positive sense, than any of the other remarkable happenings of the same year.

In 1939, Little League baseball was born.

Two teams of boys—sponsored by local companies and wearing baggy uniforms—played the first Little League baseball game on June 6, 1939, in the small rural town of Williamsport, Pennsylvania. Carl Stoltz is said to have originated the idea, so his nephews Harold "Major" Gehron (age eight) and Jimmy Gehron (age six) would have a chance to play organized ball. Necessity (once again) being the mother of invention, Stoltz recalled his own disappointment when, as a child, he could not play baseball because the older boys dominated the field, leaving the smaller ones with nothing to do but sit on the sidelines and watch. He decided that some day, he would start a league specifically for younger boys, so they could compete against each other.

The first Little League consisted of thirty boys on three teams, sponsored by Lundy Lumber, Lycoming Dairy, and Jumbo Pretzel Co. By 1989, that number had grown to 2.5 million children, and more than 7,500 programs.

Initially, the rules governing Little League baseball were the same as the adult major leagues'. The field was soon scaled down, however, to a more reasonable size for the players, with a home-plate-to-pitcher's-mound distance of forty-six feet. To make Little League safer and more competitive, Dr. Creighton Hale studied the game, and intervened to move the mound back two feet. In 1959, he invented the Radial-ribbed batting helmet used even to-day.

With our men returning home from the battlefields of WWII, Little League quickly spread across the country. In the first Little League World Series, played in 1947 in Williamsport, Pennsylvania, the Maynard Midgets beat Lock Haven, 16–7. Soon, Little League burst outside the U.S. boundaries, with Quebec entering the first foreign team to play the World Series. Little League was introduced to the Orient via South Korea in 1951 and spread with enthusiasm through the Pacific Rim. In 1957, a non-U.S. team won the Little League World Series for the first time, when a young boy named Angel Macias threw a perfect game against La Mesa from California, giving the Monterey, Mexico, team a 4–0 win.

In 1962, Japan sent the first Asian team to the Little League World Series, and five years later, West Tokyo won the title, start-ing a dominance that would continue until 1982, when, during those fifteen years, Asian teams would win the World Series pen-nant thirteen times.

Today, Little League is truly a world sport, with more than fifty-two countries offering programs. Not only has it helped bring the peoples of the planet a little closer, it has become socially innova-tive. In 1974, due to the changing social climate, girl teams were introduced to Little League via softball. In the same year, T-ball allowed six- to eight-year-olds to learn the basics of the game in a safe, noncompetitive manner.

America has always had a romance with baseball, and a soft spot in its heart for children, so President Dwight D. Eisenhower's declaration that the second week in June be known as National Little League Week was applauded across the nation. In 1964, the U.S. Congress granted Little League baseball a federal charter, making it the only sport ever to be given such an honor, even to this day. What a fitting tribute to a sport that indeed embodies the American spirit of equality and fair play for all!